"Love life and life will love you back.
Love people and they will love you back."

Arthur Rubinstein

"Love is the only sane and satisfactory answer to
the problem of human existence."

Erich Fromm

"Your task is not to seek for love, but merely
to seek and find all the barriers within yourself
that you have built against it."

Rumi

WHAT IS LOVE?
MESSAGES FROM THE HEART

LEXIE BROCKWAY POTAMKIN
ORIGINAL ART FROM PAINTINGS BY SUSAN B. HOWARD

Library of Congress Cataloging-in Publication Data

What Is Love? Messages From The Heart / [compiled by] Lexie Brockway Potamkin; Artwork by Susan B. Howard.

ISBN: 978-0-9824590-1-0 (Hardcover)

First Printing, June, 2010
Second Printing, March, 2014

Printed by Palace Printing & Design, China

I dedicate this book to my children and husband,
who have taught and shown me great love.

"There is no surprise more magical than the surprise of being loved. It is God's finger on man's shoulder."

Charles Morgan

Acknowledgments

What is Love? Love is inclusive of all people. Love is reciprocal. Love is universal.

Just as love is a reciprocal, collaborative process, this book on love would not have been possible without the participation of so many loving people from all over the globe who kindly shared their own experiences and thoughts about love. Thank you.

I am very grateful to Susan B. Howard, whose artwork inspires love, laughter and joy. A special thank you to Elliott Curson, Karla Kuban, Lisa Willison and Juan Guerrero, an amazing team whose love, support and hard work crafted this beautiful book.

To Cynthia Bourgeault, my appreciation for her brilliant mind, her loving, heartfelt teachings and wisdom.

Thank you to my husband, children, family and friends. Their steadfast love is the wind beneath my wings that allows me to fly and soar.

CONTENTS

Introduction

Who so loves believes the impossible.
Elizabeth Barrett Browning

My father always told me, "It's more important to be loving than to be right." Love is all we have. Love is all we are. Love is all there is. Socrates said, "The life unexamined is not worth living." What does this have to do with love? I believe it means we must examine our lives.

When we begin the quiet process of looking inward, a divine creativity works on our behalf and opens our hearts to love. When I move into a more vulnerable, authentic self, I connect more deeply with those around me. When my heart is open, time melts away, I lose my defenses and let my original innocence flourish.

My friend and teacher, Cynthia Bourgeault, has said many times, "In silence, God can be held close with love, with thought never." The heart, by its very nature, is spiritual and connects us to love.

What is Love? is my third book. The first two, *What is Spirit?* and *What is Peace?,* consider personal experience and meaning from people of all ages with broad ranges of vocations and avocations, people of many religions, from cultures worldwide. When we have the pleasure of sitting down and considering love's significance in so many ways, the process becomes holistic, or whole. When you see love, and give love, when love is received, there is transformation. Love begets love.

Where does love begin? Many of the great wisdom teachers speak of the limitless power we have inside us to love. Pure love and intimacy start with each of us individually. Quantum physics and psychology experts have proved that thoughts create our own reality. Hara Estroff Marano, editor-at-large of *Psychology Today,* writes:

"Self-love involves recognizing that you are constantly evolving and growing to become a more powerful and more loving being. The universe is literally made of love."

Ms. Marano states, simply: self-love is a commitment to ourselves. Think of what we do every day in the name of self-love. We exercise, eat healthy food, meditate, care for others and sleep, to name a few.

For many years I had a public relations career in New York. I loved the creative process and just going to work made me grateful and content. I was intent on supporting myself, taking care of my mom after my father died, building businesses and more. But something was missing. As young as 20, in my grief after my father passed away, I began to set patterns in burying my pain and loss.

I started to build a wall that few people could infiltrate, including myself. Back then a friend of mine, an MD, read my ayurvedic pulse and looked at me in surprise and said, "Your inherent nature is to live a contemplative life, but you've completely sidetracked your natural state and created a Type A personality."

My priorities had to change. Now I work at home and much of my time is devoted to my family. The last 20 years have represented a gradual unpacking and rewiring through self-analysis, personal growth experiences, study, contemplation and hard work in an effort to return to my natural state and true self. I try to keep in mind, always, what's important: it's the quality of the journey. I'm a combination of my learned Type A personality and my innately quiet, contemplative self. I'm a more heartfelt and present human being. I'm dedicated to learning all that I can about forgiving others, and myself when I make mistakes. I'm as faithful as time allows to my own spiritual journey, including meditation and silence. Nothing pleases the Divine more than the beauty of the unfolding of who we truly are.

One of the gifts of contemplation is that it leaves us more defenseless. My corporate life kept me more defensive. Defensiveness blocks love and deep connection to others. Bridging the gap has helped me balance my life and stay more loving.

Through travel and studies I learned about world religions, culture and customs, and that all humans and creatures deserve love and respect. I ask my children to plant the seeds of love, emphasizing that their seeds will grow and that love will spread.

Johnny Appleseed wandered barefoot in the 1700s, rescuing lost, sick animals and creating apple nurseries. In Ohio, one of his trees still thrives, a reminder of the seeds he planted, and his kind and loving ways.

True love is accepting and not demanding. Spiritually speaking, we travel from truth to truth, not untruth to untruth. Love is our birthright. However, we can miss the mark if we forget that we're part of divine love and wisdom. That includes everything and everyone on the planet.

What is divine wisdom? Slowing down, becoming quiet, listening to the still, small voice within us — sometimes called intuition, or higher self — and trusting it. We need to stay open to the wisdom of others. My awareness has moved away from "I" toward a larger vision that includes and recognizes everyone around me as a teacher. The Sanskrit word *namaste* means: I honor the divinity in you and the divinity in me. In divine wisdom, paying attention to coincidence, synchronicity and heart-felt signs may not seem meaningful at the time; but if you watch and listen, doors will open to love and learning.

My books are all subtitled *"Messages from the Heart."* I believe true love can be found when we quiet the mind and tune into our hearts. The book *Silence*, by Robert Sardello, describes silence as a "who," not an "it." Silence isn't the absence of sound, but a field of vibrant energy. Love is found somewhere in the silence that lies within us. When we move away from cognitive thinking into a quiet, still, profoundly full realm of calmness, there we find love.

I have learned to welcome stillness into my daily life through meditation. It's a pathway to becoming fully conscious. I find that meditating 20 minutes twice a day opens my heart to love more fully. When you learn a new craft, like meditation, it takes practice. Spiritual practice allows us to stay fully conscious, and more loving. Life, as we live it day in and day out, is a practice, too. If we begin each day, every morning, with a love practice, we are choosing to be lovingly aware.

When I feel an intense love for all, I have a sense of community, unity and oneness, as in the film *Avatar*: "I see you." I see who you really are, a divine loving soul yearning for more love. This unity feels sacred, holy and loving.

Love is the ultimate healer and soother. The act of placing a band-aid on my son's skinned knee heals and sooths not only him, but me. Love works in powerful ways, and sometimes we don't even realize its strength until long after a thought or an act has passed.

Most of what I learned about love came from my parents. One of my mom's favorite sayings comes from Book I of Corinthians: "And now these three remain: faith, hope, and love. But the greatest of these is love."

My mom also said, "It's the small, simple things in life that make a big difference." I gained so much knowledge from my dear, sweet mom. Love never dies because I can reclaim the wisdom and deep love my parents held for me. They radiated with love from their hearts to others. Their love lives inside me, and it's my responsibility to evoke it and reclaim it in my life.

When my children were born, it felt like I drank a love potion and found myself swimming in a deep pool of the most intimate love I had ever known. When that memory fills my heart, I feel reciprocal love for each of my children; a heart-to-heart connection. No matter what your tradition or spirituality, I believe it's possible that we can tap into this realm called love, and there we can find great compassion for one another.

I was once interviewed for a business magazine article and was asked for my definition of success. My answer was that success is the quality of the journey. Love follows the same paradigm. To me, love makes life a quality journey.

When I was a teen, I read a book called *The Cross and the Switchblade*, by David Wilkerson. It's a true story about the first five years of a priest's work in New York City as he ministered to young, disillusioned gang members. His love changes gang members' lives, thereby transforming families and communities.

Is it possible for us to create change in our own schools and neighborhoods through the power of love?

Love creates everyday miracles and heals wounded hearts.

If you ask my children what matters, they will answer, "Love!" One day they will understand, as I did after my parents' deaths, that the ultimate question we will all have to ask is how loving have we been, and how we have demonstrated love in our lives?

When a neighbor is sick, do we call on them, perhaps bring them a bowl of hot soup? When someone criticizes us and hurts our feelings, do we thank them for their observations, check our egos, get on with life and forgive our critics? Identification — ego — drops away when we shift from our minds into our hearts. Energy bound in identification is freed, and released. Real love and feelings keep us balanced. Deep love is possible if we make a clean break from egocentric habits connected with our self-worth. We all have heart-opening work to do, but we can all connect deeply into love, from our hearts. What blocks love and virtue is self-interest.

In my early teenage years, I was vying for independence. When I didn't get my way, I would pout, storm into my room, slam the door with a big bang and plop down on my bed in an overly dramatic manner typical to most teens. Ten minutes later my father would knock on the door, peek inside, and ask, "May I come in?" I would shout back, in my stormiest voice, "Go away!" He would say, "Just for one minute." He calmly walked over to me, gave me a hug, and said, "I'm sorry. Please forgive me. I love you." These words melted my heart. I'd hug him back and say, "I'm the one acting selfish, not you. You didn't do anything. I'm sorry. Please forgive me. I love you."

In this manner, my father taught me about unselfish, unconditional, non-egoic love. In my curiosity about why he apologized first, my father said, "Being loving is more important than being right." At those moments, my heart was opened by his authentic, non-egoic wisdom. I learned the true meaning of love. When we choose humility over self-importance, we move into deeper love.

We can all work on opening our hearts to this deeper more meaningful level of love. In my third semester at the Spiritual Paths

Institute of Santa Barbara, Kabir Helminski, a Sufi scholar, taught the four most transformative groups of words in altering any situation: I'm sorry, forgive me, thank you and I love you. In Kabir's teaching, I was reminded how easily my father chose love over righteousness. My father was a master in transforming any negative situation into love and understanding. I like to call him a love reclaimer.

What is your idea of love? How is it manifested in your world? When was the last time you examined a long-held grudge and gave it up, then called or wrote to that person and offered forgiveness? How did it make you feel? If we open our minds and hearts, we can find love everywhere.

Love in the moment is divine, but memories of love can sooth the soul, too. John Denver wrote a song titled "Perhaps Love." Here are his insightful words:

Perhaps love is like a resting place
A shelter from the storm
It exists to give you comfort
It is there to keep you warm
And in those times of trouble
When you are most alone
The memory of love will bring you home

Perhaps love is like a window
Perhaps an open door

It invites you to come closer
It wants to show you more
And even if you lose yourself
And don't know what to do
The memory of love will see you through

If someone close to me withdraws, I hold that person in a vision of love, projected from and through my heart, and hope that someday their heart will open more fully to love. I plant the seed and have faith that the seed will someday grow into a magnificent tree.

If I were a tree, my trunk would be Christian, my roots Hindu, Jewish, Buddhist, Native American, and Sufi. My roots support the core, and every faith keeps me loving and strong. I love rituals. Hearing the sacred sounds of Tibetan Buddhist monks is very healing for my soul. They blow conch shells, and chant. Hindus play the harmonium, a magical reed instrument. Many traditions burn incense, a sweet perfume.

Whether it's a Eucharist ceremony, a Durga Puja, a Tibetan Buddhist puja, or an inter-spiritual Zikir, I feel divine grace and love touching my soul in ritual celebrations. Hearing Hebrew chanted in a temple or Christian songs sung in Greek, Latin or Aramaic, my soul is filled with sacred sound vibrations. These sounds and ceremonies open my heart and take me to a place of deep love and connectedness.

These traditions unite at the heart level. His Holiness, the Dalai Lama, says, "Do not give up your core religion, but if you want, allow the Buddhist teachings to add to or deepen your own tradition." We can learn from everyone, and teach love by our actions. All the traditions, along with my meditative practice, offer me the nutrients I need to grow, expand and transform.

I believe it's better to look for similarities instead of differences. When we learn to love other traditions, we begin to respect and love one another. We can delight in the differences, and find a meeting place.

When I was Miss World USA, I was asked: If you could trade places with anyone, who would it be with and why? I said that person would be Helen Steiner Rice, because she was a successful businesswoman, who inspired others. She was a poet and made a difference helping others through her foundation. One of her poems reads, "Great is the power of might and mind, but only love can make us kind."

Loving memories keep us going during difficult times. My brother-in-law, Alan, holds a similar sentiment to one my mom always kept: It's the little things that are big. Alan's father, a strong-willed, self-made man, six-feet tall with a full head of salt-and-pepper hair, passed away a few years ago. After his death, Alan found an old pair of his father's shoes and kept them. During Yom Kippur, in a ceremony offering prayers for the departed, Alan wears his father's shoes to temple, keeping his loving memory alive.

Not long ago my sister, my brother and I went to the Aspen Chapel, with its striking golden stained-glass windows. This Sunday I had given flowers for the altar in memory of our mom. At some point during the service, I reached into my purse and withdrew a photograph of our smiling mom, then handed it to my siblings. I could see, in their eyes, gratitude. In our mom's teachings of love, she opened our hearts to it. Through flowers and a simple photo, my siblings and I reconnected with our mom's wisdom, and kept her love alive.

The Toltec philosopher Don Miguel Ruiz, reveals certain beliefs that rob us of joy and create suffering. In changing the negative agreements we may have with ourselves, and honoring four simple rules, we can be guided into true happiness, and love:

> *When we are impeccable with our words, we speak with integrity. We say what we mean, avoid gossip and use the power of our words in the direction of truth and love.*

> *Not taking things personally frees us from negative actions and words. Nothing anyone does is because of us. What others say and do is a projection of their own reality. When we are immune to the opinions and actions of others, we are not victims of needless suffering.*

> *Don't make assumptions. Find the courage to ask questions and to express what you really want. Communicate with others clearly to avoid misunderstandings, sadness and drama.*

> *In doing our best, always, we have to be on our toes, as life changes from minute to minute. When we lose sleep or are sick, it's hard to do our best. However, if we strive to do our utmost, even in less*

than optimal conditions, we can avoid self-judgment, self-abuse, regret and guilt. We will, instead, garner self-love, strengthening our ability to give love and to give it unconditionally.

When was the last time you sat and watched children playing in a park, gathered around a Scrabble game or laughing with their cousins at a holiday celebration? Not everyone was born to have children. Even so, we must take a few minutes each day to watch children at play. Their imaginations are powerful, and the way they dream up adventure allows them to live in the moment. Children express what they feel, and are not afraid to love. They seem to learn early that love is kind, and that kindness makes them generous and opens doors. They forgive quickly and play again. They seem to sense that even trees are made with love.

Animals are made with love. Water is made with love. What makes us feel like happy children? When we go to that place, we find our joy, innocence and compassion. Sometime, when you're playing and enjoying yourself, observe how time disappears. Honor that place. We don't want to numb our hearts. By living in our hearts, we project light and love to others.

Love puts someone else's welfare before our own. I loved taking care of my mom before she passed away, because giving to her brought love to me. Just minutes before she died, I whispered into her ear that she was the greatest mom in the world. I thanked her. She opened her eyes for a second and said, "I love you." Then, as I held her hand, she crossed over. My mom, and wisdom teacher, knew that love never dies. I miss not being able to call my mom and dad when I'm having a bad day, but I can reclaim their love by tapping into silence and calmness. I can feel them vibrationally, a loving gift.

As we move from positive intentions into loving action, we become more receptive and whole. Jerry Jampolsky wrote a classic book, *Love is Letting Go of Fear*. So many of our fears are imaginary, he says, based on faulty reasoning and thinking. As we let go of our fears, our hearts open to love. We can find love in forgiving and forgetting. My mom used to say we must practice both, that forgetting is just as important as forgiving. When we place disagreements behind us, we re-invite love and grace into our hearts and can truly begin to heal.

Our pets teach us to love unconditionally. If we're in a bad mood or begin to cry, a pet will appear and show compassion with a nudge, or by sitting down at our feet.

For centuries, animals have been used in therapeutic situations. Near our town, there's a riding camp for children with special needs. Children help feed and care for the horses, learn to ride and, in the exchange of love, become more self-sufficient, with greater confidence.

Some time ago I had a root canal, and suffered quite a lot of discomfort. I held my dog, Suzy, and was soothed by her loyalty and love. She elevated my spirit and, before I knew it, my pain was gone. Our pets are little guardian angels, giving unconditional love and watching over us when we need them most.

On December 21, 2012, the Mayan calendar marks the end of a 5,126-year era. Some say it will be a time of widespread catastrophe, perhaps the end of the world. Andrew Smith, a spiritual healer, predicts a restoration, or a "true balance between divine feminine and masculine."

Gerardo Barrios, a Mayan medicine man, began his spiritual journey when he was 13 with a Mayan master shaman. He spent 20 years traveling to villages in Guatemala, Mexico, Belize, El Salvador and Honduras, interviewing nearly 600 Mayan timekeepers.

He writes: "We are now in a transition period called the cycle of the merge of the dark and the light. The cycle of the light will come in full force on 12/21/2012. Mother Earth as a living entity will transcend to another level or frequency of consciousness and a new and special era will begin. This era will be positive. The times are here for total brotherhood and sisterhood. Different philosophies and different races must begin to weave together all knowledge to create the tapestry of harmony and balance."

I like to think of that milestone as a dawning age of light, when we can more fully realize our capacity for deep, meaningful love and find divinity in the world.

Jonas, Lee and Herman Salk came from unassuming Russian-Jewish immigrant parents with humble backgrounds. Doran and Daniel Salk lacked formal educations, but were determined to see their sons succeed. All three boys grew up to become important leaders in their fields: Jonas Salk developed the polio vaccine, and refused to patent his invention; he had no desire to profit from its uses. Herman became a veterinarian, working in third-world countries and teaching people how to care for their animals. He said, "A vet has to feel what the dog feels. When I get a patient with a tense belly, I find my belly getting tense, too." Lee was a renowned child psychologist and author of numerous books, including *Familyhood: Nurturing the Values That Matter*. He was an expert on family relationships: social change, domestic strife and changing family patterns.

When I asked Lee how his parents produced three amazing boys who grew into such extraordinary men, he told me a story. The strength of three words — I love you — led their upbringing. Each night before bed, the Salk parents hugged their sons and told them how much they loved them. As an adult, when Lee was about to catch a train that would launch him into World War II, Daniel Salk threw his arms around Lee and told him how much he loved him. While other fathers were shaking their sons' hands and telling them to be careful, Daniel's words were simple and powerful: "I love you." Is there any doubt how much influence love had on these three astonishing minds and careers?

In compiling *What is Love?* we were fortunate to find an incredible variety of people from all walks of life with intriguing insights, experiences and beliefs. All are part of the intricate tapestry of love, and we cherish their contributions.

Susan B. Howard's paintings, as you will see, are a stunning complement to words of love. Her images are colorful and complex, yet uncomplicated, whimsical and joyous. For me, her work evokes innocence and brings to mind some of my own memories of childhood enchantment. As you page through Susan's wondrous creations, maybe you will allow them to take you back to lovely younger days: tree climbing, an owl sighting, beading a bracelet. The simple act of remembering enjoyment and wonder keeps love alive and blooming.

The Paramahansa Yogananda said, "To describe love is very difficult, for the same reason that words cannot fully describe the flavor of an orange. You have to taste the fruit to know its flavor. So with love." Perhaps the most complete definition of love comes from I Corinthians 13:4-7. We all know it: "Love is patient, love is kind. It does not envy, it does not boast, it is not proud. It is not rude, it is not self-seeking, it is not easily angered, it keeps no record of wrongs. Love does not delight in evil but rejoices with the truth. It always protects, always trusts, always hopes, always perseveres."

Each of us is a beacon of love and light. Let there be more of it in the world. Divine love lives within each of us. Walk in love. Let's live our lives in love. Love bears all things, believes all things, hopes all things and endures all things.

The very essence of our being is love.

Lexie Brockway Potamkin

Before you read on, take a moment to look into your own heart and soul, and answer the question:

WHAT IS LOVE?

"In an extremely materialistic world, love is the feeling that reminds us that we are indeed spiritual beings.

Love is the light that shines through the darkness of judgment and fear."

Adriana de Moura, Art dealer

"Love is a contract that never ends."

Alex Sidi, Age 10

"Love is when my soul recognizes something in yours, and remembers all that is yet to come."

Abby Schaffer, Musician, artist, student

"Perhaps, at the core of happiness, joyfulness and bliss, love breaks through barriers, travels across continents and dances through nerve impulses to excite neurotransmitters.

My guess is that love happens when the mind, heart and spirit pulse in perfect harmonic ecstasy. When there is love, there can be peace.

Love may best be determined by each observer's perception, through the lens of experience.

The inner and outer expression of love takes many forms: subtle and quiet; explosive, expressed or unexpressed; selfless or selfish; conscious or beneath consciousness.

Observe the love expressed by a dog for its human partner. And observe love transformed into unconditional dedication, commitment and acceptance.

Love can morph into an expression of passion, or ease into the long-term comfort of complacency.

Love is a perceived sensation that spans the universe through the hearts and minds of its inhabitants."

Alicia Sirkin, Founder and Director, Sirkin Creative Living Center

"Love is the warm feeling you get in your core when your phone rings and you hear it's your daughter calling, and she just wanted to chat.

When you wake up in the middle of the night, can't get back to sleep and your husband rubs your temples till you fall asleep — that's love.

It's never just one thing; it's all of the little things you do for your loved one, or your loved one does for you."

Amy Elder, Teacher

"Love is taking a deep interest in the needs and feelings of another.

It involves investing time and mental and physical energies in their needs and in carefully assisting them or guiding them.

To love, you care for their needs, and not your own. But you don't do for others what they are capable of doing for themselves.

Love means giving others support, encouragement, respect and freedom to grow."

Angel Graham, Teacher

"Love is acceptance of a person as he or she is."

Angela Timashev, Small business owner

"Love is more than a feeling of happiness and joy in the moment.

Love is a decision that you will care about the other person, God or country.

One moment we can feel ecstasy for the object of our feelings; the next moment, despair or hatred. What actually changed isn't the person or object of our attention, but ourselves. Our decision to love must be rooted in a constant belief in the value of what or whom we love.

When my mother died, I was angry with God, and hated Him. But after those feelings subsided, my feelings reverted back to my core belief system.

A persecuted Jew in the Warsaw ghetto wrote how God was doing everything possible to cause him to turn his back on religion, but he affirmed that his belief and love would not change, regardless. One minute I'm upset with my partner — the next minute he's wonderful. Love transcends all this and ultimately holds fast through the rainstorm until the sun shines again."

Abigail Rubin, Music teacher

"I think of you — I smile.
I want to protect you.
I cry if you are in pain.
I can't be happy if you are not.
I miss your touch.
I think of you again. And I smile."

Alan Potamkin, Businessman

"Love is the positive energy that we feel in our souls.

We express love in different ways any time we intensify that positive energy.

It is the spark of the beginning, the essence of being — the mother, the son, the daughter, the family, the friend, the animals, the universe, nature."

Anna Maria Torres, International flight attendant

"Love is patient; love is kind. Love isn't envious, boastful, arrogant or rude. It doesn't insist on its own way. It isn't irritable or resentful. It doesn't rejoice in wrongdoing, but rejoices in the truth. It bears all things, believes all things, hopes all things and endures all things." — Corinthians

Chaya Herzberg, Pediatric optometrist

"I recently underwent a sea of change that redefined my concept of what love is. I lost someone most precious to me, and in what seems now to be a sort of divine gift, gained a greater understanding of what it means to be of service, in the service of love.

When I was two months pregnant with my daughter, Lola Jane, I found out my mother Barbara had terminal uterine cancer. She was the family historian, and lived her life in the service of others. The service of love and helping, you might say. She liked good wine, but never spent money on other material things. She wasn't rich, but she had abundant gifts of wisdom and the kind of love she taught me to pass on.

She counseled students and strangers alike on love, relationships, unwanted pregnancies and abuse.

She turned her helping heart and mind to me countless times throughout our time together, and tried when I was a journalist and producer in my 20s to tell me her family's stories.

Sadly, I didn't listen. Like many people that age, I was disinterested. I was focused on my career and finding a mate. Knowing about my mother's condition and the fact that her life was to be abbreviated hit me like a Mack truck.

I spent much of that year desperately trying to capture her thoughts, voice and face on different media before she died just six short months later. In the end, I failed to get all I could have, had I been paying attention earlier. I felt cheated. My daughter wouldn't have Grandma Bobbie's wonderful stories at her fingertips. I knew this could have been avoided. It was my greatest regret.

But, out of this regret came the inspiration to help others benefit from the terrible mistake I made. One wintry day in Ann Arbor, Michigan, confounded by my loss, exhausted as a new mother, confused about what next to do with my life, I got an answer in the subtlest of ways. Walking down a frozen street, a friend shared a story about her formative years. She told me about being sent by her grandparents to boarding school in Switzerland — away from an abusive and troubled family. Although we had been friends for years, I had never heard this story; I wondered if her three children had heard it.

Soon after, infant in arms, I founded a company to pass on stories for generations to come.

And so, as my mom gave her life to the service of love, I try to do the same. I evangelize to audiences — particularly younger people. I implore them to care now, not later."

Alli Joseph, Founder and President, Seventh Generation Stories

"Love is one of the most important attributes assigned to mankind.

You can't see it. You can't touch it. You can't hear it.

The capacity to love is a gift from above.

Love is a feeling of well-being in your heart.

It's a feeling you are willing to share as you look for the same in others."

Amy Dowling, Reading specialist

✿

"At 46, I'd never been married or even lived with a man. I searched for love and security my whole life, and I finally found love through a dating service on the internet.

What is love on the internet? It's the perfect fantasy. It's everything you ever wished and hoped for. The man tells you exactly what you hoped and dreamed about on the phone. You meet and sparks fly. He's everything you ever wanted and, you are everything he has ever fantasized about.

He wants to live with you, pay off your debt, promise you a future of security, intimacy, happiness, great sex and an incredible lifestyle.

And to top it all off, he tells you he loves you every day. And you are finally able to give all the love you had stored in your heart."

Dawn Rosenmayr, Associate director of philanthropy

"Love is many different things. As a mother I find that it's tough letting my 14-, 17-, and 20-year-old sons go to find themselves. But love enables them to do it.

It's being supportive by attending their sports games and school activities. It's playing cards or board games with them, sitting down to a family dinner and reading to them at night.

It's watching them make choices you don't want them to make, and then helping them see that every choice they make has a consequence — good or bad. It's experiencing pure joy at their successes and heart-wrenching pain when they're hurt.

As a daughter, it's being gentle with aging parents, taking time to talk to them and listening to what they have to say.

As a teacher, it's helping students reach their potential by guiding them to find within the greatness they can achieve if they believe in themselves. As a lover, it's believing and sharing activities together.

It's doing what you believe and know what is best for you — taking care of your health, having a positive attitude and surrounding yourself with good, healthy, positive people.

It's having wonderful friends to share your life with."

Bernadette Campoli, High school teacher

"Love is when you know that no matter what happens, your family and friends will never forget you and you will never forget them.

Love is when you can read with your family in front of a fire on a winter day.

Love is when you can smile and enjoy life. In your lifetime you want to be able to walk into your home and feel comfort and warmth.

Love isn't when you say hi, and see your kids for an hour a day. It's when you have family dinners. It's when everything in your life matters.

Life is love. Love is life."

Arley Breen Gordon, Age 11

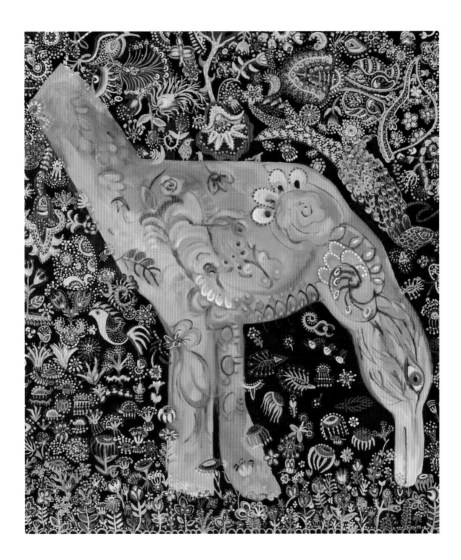

"Love is the basis of all manifestation, be it the body, the emotions or nature. Love is all. There is no judgment in love as it is free and without blame.

Love is the only thing that can be believed in, as it is the strength and fortitude for which everything is connected to.

Love cannot be looked up in the dictionary as there is nothing to compare it to.

We can experience it through positive virtues such as compassion, kindness, gentleness and patience.

When we surrender to this love we know how precious we are as we are."

Barbara Eisenberg, Shiatsu practitioner

"Love is an abstract concept that becomes concrete when individuals utilize it at any given point in their lives.

Love is relative to the individual who demonstrates it as well as the person who receives it.

Love, as it is conceptualized, is static. But the notion of love ebbs and flows.

In other words, love is situational, circumstantial and loosely defined."

Bernice Henry, New teacher coach

"There are many types and expressions of love, and they can be described in three categories:

Romantic love is passionate, sexual and inspiring. It's the type of love you feel for another person that makes your heart yearn, your spirit sing and your body tingle. It drives the life force and it fuels creativity. It can make time and reality seem to stand still. It feels blissful and can change how you view yourself and the world.

Nurturing love is unconditional and adoring. It's the type of love that cherishes another person in the deepest manner. It's boundless and enduring. This is the type of love you feel for your child, a dear friend or a family member. It evokes a caring that is selfless and pure. It's a love that makes you happy just because the other person exists.

Universal love is altruistic and inclusive. It's the type of love you feel for something larger than yourself or your personal existence. It's an appreciation of nature, humanity, art, beauty, ideas and all aspects of life itself. It can feel like a holy experience. It has the capacity to bring all things together and heal what is wrong.

It's a love that can be shared by all and reflects grace itself."

Brigitt Rok, Psychologist

✿

"Love is the sparkle in your eye that lights up the world around you, and makes others smile when they see you."

David Standig, Gold Life Master bridge teacher

"Love is another one of God's awesome gifts. He bestows it upon us with no conditions attached. To love another is to imitate, in a small way, the infinite love God has for all of us.

Studies have proven the basic need of all human beings, in order to grow into well-adjusted people, is love.

Who better to imitate than the all-loving God who created us and keeps us in existence."

Barbara A. Steinmetz, Teacher

"First of all, love is God. All love emanates from Him. When we are open to His love, we can love ourselves and others immeasurably.

Love is a myriad of things but fundamentally it's a dynamic commitment to act on God's love in us for others. It's a decision to commit to caring for and showing charity to another or others.

Love can be romantic feelings; a fire and passion to give and receive unconditionally — always guarding the respect and dignity we owe one another.

Love is hard work. It takes constant communication, nurturing and clarifying.

Love is a gift."

Bert Chilson, Reverend

"Love is the energy that supports 'all that is' in the universe.

It's the absolute truth of both who we are and what we are created from.

Love is everything good in the world and the energy that supports the perfection of every experience we may deem bad. Every intimate moment with another, ourselves and our spirit — that is love.

Every moment of change, growth and realization — that is love.

Every perspective that takes the road of total acceptance, compassion and unity — that is love. Every moment of appreciation, gratitude and wonder — that is love.

Every connected feeling of our true selves and that of every one and everything around us — that is love. Coming back to a place of honor, time and time again — that is love.

Love is the magic that makes all dreams come true. It's the fabric of our being and the life of the creator in action."

Carolyn Golbus, Singer, songwriter

"Love is when your golden retriever runs to you, sits down and puts her paw on your foot.

Love is when you fall off your thoroughbred mare and she's careful not to step on you. Love is when a child hugs you — just because.

Love is the connection between all living things."

Chip Comins, Producer, director

"Love is the humility, focus and respect of self, and therefore others.

A former acquaintance, and now a close friend, told me a year after the fact that she was operated on for cancer at the same time that my father committed suicide. She said that I had 'enough on my plate.'

Love is having been able to pass that on to a lifelong friend by not telling her when I was diagnosed with a brain tumor — shortly after her husband had been.

Love was my Parisian mother joining the French resistance, despite having a fairly uninterrupted life under the Nazi occupation.

Love turned my mother, who was Catholic, into marrying my father, whose mother was Jewish.

My mother was subjected to repeated torture by the Nazis in France and Germany before they put her and 45,000 other women in the Ravensbruck concentration camp.

Love is the Allied Forces trading my mother for captured German officers shortly before the end of the war. That undoubtedly saved her life.

Love isn't what we experience when United States senators voted — as they did in November, 2007 — to condone America's use of torture, at the very time they had their best opportunity to stop it. That senators of Jewish descent were part of that bloc is obscene.

Love is allowing people to change.

Love is my grandfather giving away everything he inherited.

Love is my beloved Jack Russell terrier allowing me the space and the opportunity for me to express my love."

Christopher English Walling, Jewelry designer

19

"Love is like a roller coaster. It can go as high as a shooting star and burn out fast as it falls to earth.

It can be happy and scary at the same time.

Pure love exists in the touch of a child's hand, their first smile and word. True love is one that lasts a lifetime, that sticks around during the ups and down of life.

Love is many things to many people, but the love that you keep in your heart will never let you down. It'll be with you till the very end, and that is the best kind of love.

The love of oneself."

Barbara Zohlman, Executive Director, Drug Free Youth in Town

"Love is the purest reflection of oneness in our present reality and beyond this world. It transcends space and time.

I believe we are all interconnected and born with a purpose. Each of us is a piece of the puzzle in this intricately beautiful mosaic of life.

Love is the key to unlock hearts and join each of us by creating a bridge of interconnected hope for the present and future generations. We have the capacity to establish peace through love within ourselves and in the world around us.

By recognizing the beauty in each other and ourselves, we become mirrors reflecting one another. Unification is established through an appreciation of others, the environment and ourselves. Through grace and gratitude, light shines through as love.

Authentic leadership should link the mind with the heart in regard to communication, collaboration and cooperation for humanity. It's about realizing the importance of taking responsibility for oneself to establish balance inside and out.

There is an awakening to remember that within the stillness of oneself, spirit is ever-present, softly emanating the true essence of love. May we all experience heaven on earth within us and around us manifested in peace, love and happiness."

Dee Jensen, Founder, WIN Health Institute

"Love is passion and excitement. Love makes the heart beat faster. Love is having laughter in your life."

Kenneth Elkind, Investments

"Love is emotion that overwhelms you and can change your life forever."

John Bruno, Automobile executive

"Love is truth, respect and consideration."

John "Cha Cha" Ciarcia, Actor, wine importer

"Love is giving of yourself, to everyone you meet, and expecting nothing in return. That can also be said about couples who feel butterflies in their hearts when seeing that other person.

On a larger scale, love is doing everything you can to improve life for all of the citizens of the world. It's believing that humankind is good, and deserves the best of everything we have to offer."

Eric Jennings, Art education

"Love is the most valuable possession, yet it isn't for sale. It's what most people seek, yet it's constantly there. It can be experienced in various forms:

Love for one's self.

Love for other people.

Love for what we do.

Love for life.

Love isn't a destination. It's a medium to get there. It's the true essence of all human beings.

You must start with love to end with love. If you want to grow professionally, financially, emotionally and spiritually, love has to be included in every part of the process. Only then will the outcome will be better than expected.

Love is the spice of life. Without it, our experience on earth would be bland. Love is the key ingredient to enjoy every day."

Cecilia Elizalde, Journalist, producer

"Love is when two souls connect in a very special way and feel the depth of each other's being.

Love that is as deep as the ocean, and as clear as the purest water.

It is everlasting and never demanding.

Love always wants happiness and never sorrow. It's always considerate, kind, caring, affectionate, respectful and tolerant.

Ahh, but oh so rare."

Cindi Paradise Acquarole, Teacher

"There are different kinds of love. Love in a relationship is unconditionally accepting someone regardless of their faults.

Love for your child, or children. Making a commitment to feel their joy and pain for the extent of your life. It is breastfeeding them as babies, sharing their joys and sorrows throughout their lifelong journey and always being there to lend a helping hand.

There's love for your siblings: being able to forgive and move on.

Love for your patients: treating them as you would like to be treated — like family — and listening to their pain both with your ears and your heart.

Then there's love for humankind: introducing one to the love of God, for God is love."

Dawn Hawthorne, Location consultant

"Love is reaching out beyond yourself to another person. It's about caring for another so much that you would do anything for that person's benefit and well-being.

Love is still being able to see all that is good and beautiful in your child even when times are difficult. (One of our teenage sons is dyslexic and there have been many trying moments, especially now that he is a teen).

Love is having that feeling no matter what. That no matter how trying or how scary or how difficult things become, you commit to maintain and even enhance your relationship with your spouse.

It's when you truly believe that the only thing that would be worse than going through the difficult times with your spouse would be trying to go through it without them.

Love is knowing all the faults and quirks of your loved ones and loving them in spite of it, or maybe because of it.

And it's knowing that your husband and kids feel the same way about you."

Connie Ryan, Mom

"Love is what makes life livable. It's the most important emotion in life. Love is the power in us that allows us to make things possible that seem impossible to accomplish.

Love diminishes fear."

Cindy Martin, Teacher

"Love is commitment to the welfare of another person. It's a willingness to take responsibility for that person; to help them grow in love and responsibility.

It's work, but it's rewarding work. It involves fidelity as well as joy and suffering.

Love is a response to others loving us — because being loved frees us to risk the suffering that's involved in extending ourselves to love others."

Christine Gudorf, Professor

⁂

"For me, the most profound love I have ever felt is the unconditional love I feel for my daughter.

Don't get me wrong. I love my husband, family and friends dearly, but romantic and platonic love can hold a candle to the way I feel about my child. I love her so much that it makes me feel frightened and vulnerable at times.

She brings me greater joy than I ever thought would be possible. When she rushes up to me and tells me that she loves me, it feels better than anything in the world.

I constantly pray for her health and joy and safety. My relationship with her is by far the most important one in my life."

Darcy Roane, Mom

"The opposite of love is not hate, it's indifference. The opposite of art is not ugliness, it's indifference. The opposite of faith is not heresy, it's indifference.

And the opposite of life is not death, it's indifference."

Elie Wiesel

"You learn to speak by speaking, to study by studying, to run by running, to work by working; and just so, you learn to love by loving. All those who think to learn in any other way deceive themselves."

Saint Francis de Sales

"We must develop and maintain the capacity to forgive. He who is devoid of the power to forgive is devoid of the power to love. There is some good in the worst of us and some evil in the best of us. When we discover this, we are less prone to hate our enemies."

Martin Luther King, Jr.

"Love is the pure stream of energy that projects from our solar plexus and connects us with all other forms of life within the universal intelligence.

It's the source of purity upon which we must base our consciousness while on the planet. This needs to be often given and received to sustain our connection to oneness.

From birth, life and death, it's the one constant that we are all looking to attain from our spirituality in daily living.

Love is in everything all the time. We need to slow down to admire the beauty that is within us and around us at all times."

David Jensen, Sports chiropractor

"Love is a feeling of warmth that represents itself in many ways. There are many different types of love.

Love is meant for the living, not things. Loving a friend, a spouse, a pet, a mom. They have similar characteristics, yet different ones, as well. When I feel loved I feel connected in a special way and there's a feeling of safety that allows me to be myself, with no pretenses.

Love is wonderful."

Deborah Margulies, Professional school counselor

"Love is deserving and gracious. It's the essence of the heart's shape. It's ebullient and elated, joyful and caring.

Love provides the space to access your highest self, and the drive to achieve your dreams.

Love is motivation, an anchor. It is reason when the world seems awry. It is steady balance and a dependable guide. It's acceptance, peace of mind and passion. It's wise and knowing, confident and comfortable.

Love is nurturing. It isn't obsessive, stifling or selfish.

Love is abundant and unlimited.

It's the reason the sunset appears extra special. It's that radiant glow at breakfast. It's going that inexplicable extra mile.

Love is fairy dust rounding magical moments.

Love evolves over time. It enriches our lives in immeasurable ways. Love is all that matters."

Debra Riggs, Business development and strategy

"Love is finding someone who makes you feel alive and safe all at the same time."

Kristin Welker, Television anchor, reporter

"Love is caring for someone, forgetting about yourself and concentrating on needs that are present in life.

The very beauty of love is displayed in the fuchsia color of a crepe myrtle tree.

The love I know is gained from a powerful love of God. It is the air I breathe, my daily bread and giving words of encouragement.

It's transferring positive energy to motivate bright new teachers and children."

Deborah Victoria Williams, New teacher coach

꽃

"Life is so fragile and short that each miraculous being should know the feeling of love and being loved, of feeling safe and powerful, of being a co-creator of the magic in everyday life.

If everyone had the ability to see and understand the beauty and kindness of our planet, the world would be cared for in a reciprocal relationship. This little piece of rock in a giant universe supplies all our physical needs, and that is love.

A higher power supplies our mental and emotional needs. That, too, is love.

Love is attempting to tolerate what we view as the shortcomings of others when we are unable to see that they are they are doing the best they can with the knowledge they have gathered at this point in time."

Diana Lee, Psychologist

"Love is putting everything behind so you can be with that special person. It's leaving your family, friends, food, country and language — everything you are accustomed to — and traveling 9,000 miles to make a new life with him.

It's sitting on a small chair, but making space so he can sit with you.

Love is the first time you see the little face of your newborn. It's a connection between souls. It's giving space to your kids and letting them grow into their own personas, even when you think your way is the right way. It's letting them make their own mistakes.

Love is letting your parents treat you as a child, even though you have been an adult for the longest time.

Love is to help the injured and to try to take the pain away and make them feel better.

It's to give hope where there is none, and comfort where there is sadness.

Love is making the best out of your experience in this world."

Caterina Gibson, Hotel administrator

33

"Nothing is better than love. It can be expressed in so many ways...from a kind word to the most passionate of kisses. Spoken or unspoken doesn't matter when love is conveyed.

Loving thoughts are always understood. And no matter how love is given, it is received with that unique, warm, tingling feeling.

The more love you give the more love you get. Love is the greatest gift in the world."

Steven Neckman, Estate jewelry, diamond dealer

"Love is seeing unique, intrinsic value in an object. But, falling in love is a different concept. Being in love with a person is to be hypnotized or mesmerized by a person's way of being; to be in love is to see the totality of your desires encapsulated in one individual.

Love is that mysterious attraction that makes your heart melt just by glancing at the person. It's when time stops and makes the moments between you and your beloved eternally present."

Elizabeth Perez, Student

"Love is surrounding yourself with beautiful people and prayer. Love is forgiveness and not being afraid to say, 'I love you,' to those around you. It's showing your soul and wearing your heart on your sleeve. It's giving truly of yourself and all that you are and all you have, realizing that material possessions have little spiritual meaning.

Love is that amazing feeling you have when you look into the eyes of your children, and connecting with your soul mate on that incredible intimate level. It's closing your eyes and seeing that beam of light.

Love is not being afraid."

Deborah M. Madsen, Personal trainer

"A baby's smile, slowly spreading it's full sweetness, like a sunrise.
A dog's head resting in my lap with a contented sigh.
A mountain's stillness touching my soul's ancient memories.
My mother's tears gently kissing her lovely cheeks as she watches her daughters, granddaughters and great-granddaughters cooking, dancing and laughing together.

The surging of my heart when reading the words of great masters.
The shining rainbow at the death of my best friend.

The knowing, the constant knowing, that this life is sacred, and that love is the greatest gift."

Ellen Marie Porr, Massage therapist

"When I met my beloved husband nearly 40 years ago I was immediately attracted to his soulful brown eyes and easy smile. He showed me what love was through kindness, support, listening and laughing. There wasn't a day that we didn't express, 'I love you.' We always hugged and kissed first thing in the morning and the last thing at night.

It felt wonderful to feel so secure. We found joy in the simplest things and truly enjoyed spending time together. But we also supported one another in separate activities and interests.

He passed away over four years ago, and I miss him every day. But I see him in the faces of our children, and especially in the two new baby granddaughters that will come to know their grandfather through photographs and stories.

When you enjoy the feeling of being cherished by another, I believe that you have experienced true love."

Diane Landsberg, Executive Director, Non-Violence Project, USA

᎒

"Love is our true nature. Love gives us the freedom to be fascinated with our differences and be grateful for our multitude of similarities.

Our loving essence has no boundaries. This love doesn't perish, betray or leave.

To love yourself — as you are this moment, without judgment, and with kindness and compassion — is an art."

Ganga Ma Dickenson, Author, teacher, baker.

"Love is like jumping into a new book. When we fall in love, we're taken in by the picture on the cover, the glossy illustration of the handsome man and beautiful woman on the front looking into the other's eyes. As we turn the pages and both of the partners are still there, the love is growing.

As we get to know the characters in each other's lives, it heightens the love. As we learn this person's idiosyncrasies, pet peeves and favorite things, we feel more attached and secure.

As we continue on to the end of the book, not wanting to put it down, we hope the two lovers work out a way to overcome problems that come their way.

We crave a happy ending in our own lives. We work hard at finding and sustaining love. And once you do it's sure to be a read you'll never forget."

Dorie Lynne Clayman, Teacher

"Loving is extracting oneself from the noise in order to be there to listen to nature and enjoy this beautiful paradise.

Love is an extension and expression of the best in every being in this universe. How privileged we are to be able to feel it and express it with actions and in words."

Dr. Emma Trollerud, Professor

"Love is unselfish. It is wanting what is best for someone because you want them to be happy and successful.

Love is helping, listening and caring for those around us. It is understanding there's no need for something in return; the fact that we have made that individual's life better is acknowledgment enough for our efforts.

Love is seeing the beauty in all that is around us and in people. Everyone has something about them that is wonderful and beautiful; sometimes it's hard to see, but with love and acceptance we can see it clearly.

Love is opening up, allowing others into your most sensitive parts, and trusting that they will nurture what you are sharing. Love is what makes us smile, laugh and glow.

Love is children, their laughter, their innocence and most of all their ability to be honest beyond all means."

Enoelia Zaldivar, Teacher

"Love can manifest itself in many ways: love for a spouse, children and parents. Love for your fellow man. Love for God. But that's not a definition. Can it really be defined?

It is a feeling, a bond that connects people in different ways throughout your life and others. It's talked about, sung about, written about and read about. But that isn't defining it. Perhaps it can't be defined, only experienced.

Without it, we would be nothing."

Jeane Milligan, Catholic school teacher

"Whether it's toward a spouse, a parent, a child, a relative or a dear friend, there are undeniably similar characteristics to what we call love, what we know as love, and what we feel as love.

Love is that unwavering feeling of attachment and devotion that cannot be broken, no matter how often it is tested. Certainly you can make a different list for what love is with each variety of love, but in the end, it is truly unquantifiable. You look in the eyes of those you love, and you just know.

Love is a feeling so strong, it can be conjured from memory, so when a person isn't near, or no longer, you can simply imagine that look, that smile, that touch, that warmth, and the feeling of love arrives.

So what is love? It is the greatest gift. A gift we turn to often, a feeling like none other, a feeling so thankfully limitless."

Gerard Schwarz, Music Director, Seattle Symphony Orchestra

Jody Schwarz, Flutist

"There are infinite degrees of love. The love of a woman for a man, the love of a parent for their child, the love of friends, the love of family, the love of country and the love of all humankind.

True love is putting another above oneself.

Love is in the heart of God. We reach heaven through love, since God is love. One could not believe in God if one did not find love on earth. Love is given to us so that we can see a soul. Love is letting go of all ego and fear. Love is respect, kindness and caring for others. It's always being there for others in good times and bad, no matter how inconvenient it might be.

It is through loving eyes that we see a universe that is beautiful and filled with peace. Love is not judging others.

Love is tolerance and forgiveness."

Donna Lundgren-Wiedinmyer, Real estate investor

"Love is knowing it's better to care than be cared for, better to love than be loved and better to understand than be understood.

Love is humility without humiliation.

Love is patience and more patience.

Love is letting go of resentments.

Love is forgiving, even if not being forgiven.

Love is forgiving, even if not always forgetting.

Love is gratitude for the small things."

Doug Erpf, Manager, long-term recovery residence

"Love is getting up early for work, entering the bathroom, closing the door and then turning on the light.

When your spouse is sleeping in, not putting your socks on while sitting on the bed.

Buying the low fat, tasteless ice cream because your spouse is watching calories.

Taking turns going to chick flicks and stupid science-fiction action movies.

Holding your spouse's forehead as he or she regurgitates into your favorite Dolphin team collector's wastebasket, signed by Mercury Morris.

Going to those ridiculously boring, three-hour-long, professional rubber-chicken dinners because your spouse was a board officer nine years ago.

Love is about compromise and sacrifice, and acknowledging these two efforts in your lover."

Eliot Pearlson, Rabbi

✿

"Love is wanting others to be happy.

The love of a parent for their child is like seeing a rainbow for the first time. It's like opening a door and seeing a new world in color that was previously only black and white."

Kevom Arrow, Museum registrar, exhibition coordinator

"The Beatles said that all you need is love. Who knew how right they were! But the love they spoke of wasn't perfect. Perfect love comes from God. We can only know perfect love from Him.

Mankind's love is fine but it isn't perfect. This is why we hurt in this life. The best part is that His love is free and there's no catch.

I love that. That's why faith in God is the only way to know true, perfect, unconditional love.

Who could want anything more?"

Jeanette Scally, Teacher

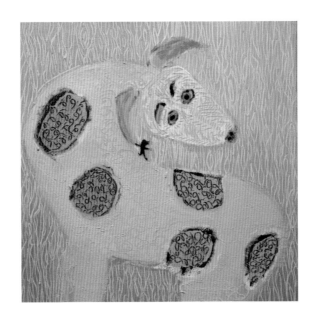

"Love can't be explained in words. It can only be experienced. It has no beginning or end. It's our true essence and the building blocks of our spiritual being. Love shines and is fully expressed when our spiritual nature is revealed. It's innately unconditional. It creates, shares, gives, and is always unselfish.

The human plight is the reconciling of our spiritual nature in a human experience. The more spiritually aware we become, the more we love; and the less spiritually aware we are, the more we fear. Life is about loving more and fearing less."

Fernando J. Valverde, MD, Associate Dean,
FIU College of Medicine

"Love is an uncertainty in one's life. If you haven't been nurtured and loved as a child, an adolescent or an adult, it is difficult to give or share with others.

Love can cause pain and joy. It's the most difficult thing for some, while others seem to have it constantly and take it for granted.

It's the backdrop for whom we became as a person. It defines one's outlook in life. Love is best when you love God, because this makes loving others easier.

Love is wonderful. It's my hope that we all experience the gift of love."

Francine Stanback, Teacher

"Love is unequivocal respect for your partner — when you treat your partner with even better manners than you would your parents, elders or strangers.

You never take advantage of your partner, even when you know their weaknesses. You always try to understand your partner's point of view and motivations.

Love is understanding that partners are imperfect and make mistakes. Love encourages individual growth, humility, forgiveness and compassion.

Love is the willingness to meet halfway. Love means we are willing to make sacrifices to support our partner.

Love is a shared idea of a common future, filled with activities and plans to be accomplished together."

Karen Cox, Operations analyst

"Love is the nectar of life."

David Taylor, Videographer

"Love is someone who will stay with you and trust you, no matter what."

Homeless person, New York City

"Love is that feeling you constantly have in the back of your mind— are they ok? Are they happy?

It's looking up at them as they appear on stage in a choral performance and see the smiles on their faces — and you experience joy. Or, when they win a tough game of tennis and they're so thrilled that you become thrilled.

It's as if there's that constant bond between you. You feel what they feel, and their happiness is more important to you than anything else."

Joe LaVecchia, Investments

"Love is the logos of life. It's the incarnation of the very source of creation. It is the essence and intention of being. Love is the ground of life and the goal of life.

The author of the Epistle of John states; 'Let us love one another; for love is of God, and the one who loves is born of God and knows God.' No one has ever seen God; if we love one another, God abides in us and God's love is perfected in us.

The one who abides in love abides in God and God abides in the one who loves. I often affirm in the marriage celebration: as God considers us each free and unique, so too shall we respect each other.

Our real task is not to be alike but to be together, not to mold one another but to receive one another, not to change the other but to abide with one another. It is through this accent of acceptance that we will truly fulfill love's purpose.

It is always through our giving that we will gain. The more we let each one be, the closer we shall become. As God loves us for who we are, so too shall we.

God is love and we are to love God and one another. Nothing more, nothing less! This is it. This is love."

Gregg R. Anderson, Chaplain, Aspen Chapel

"Love is a universal feeling of joy. It's one of the most poignant and ubiquitous emotions known to humankind, and yet the most difficult to define.

It can be compared to admiration, appreciation, acceptance or fondness.

It can be displayed between a mother and child, or found while experiencing the awe-inspiring wonders of nature.

It's a sense that you want to safeguard something. Protect it. Something holy, mystical, divine and supernatural.

Love is sometimes rare and fleeting or all-encompassing. It can be accompanied by feelings of peace and calm or exhilaration and excitement. You can receive it from people, places and life experiences.

It's the very essence of life itself. It's eternal, timeless, breathtaking and mysterious. A heavenly, blissful feeling of perfection."

Erin Frazee, Conservationist

"Love is unconditional and non-judgmental. It's a journey two people take together — exploring one another, places, people, experiences, good times, tough times, happy times, sad times.

Love is a way of growing, and treasuring every minute together until we leave this wonderful world and move on to the next.

And even in the next world I believe we will be together again."

Jill Goudie, Teacher, personal trainer

"When I love someone I feel connected to them spiritually, and that gives me an intense feeling of joy.

When I see their faults, I feel empathy for them and it makes me love them more. There are people I meet and instantly share a loving connection. At times I care more about their well-being than my own. It's an enormous relief to not feel so concerned about myself, and be more concerned about my family and friends.

I love the vicarious happiness of watching and feeling someone else be happy. The love I feel makes me feel actively engaged in life and connected to the whole of existence.

Loving animals is also an enormous source of happiness for me. I often look into an animal's eyes and see the same pure spirit that I see in a newborn's eyes. As a counselor, when I listening to people's stories I feel more engaged in life.

Love makes me feel spiritually connected to the world. It takes me outside myself."

Geraldine Morel, High school counselor

"To me, love is allowing your partner to reach their fullest potential and letting that stretch you — even if it hurts.

It's being patient with each other in order to understand how to heal each other's pain."

Gena Stewart, Higher education administrator

"Love is an uncontrollable force that takes control of your every feeling."

Richard "Bo" Dietl, Former NYC detective, actor, movie producer

"The men who have received the Congressional Medal of Honor exemplify love. Love is giving up your life for your fellow man.

When I stand before God, he will know where my heart has been. Love is forgiving unconditionally. Perhaps the ultimate act of love is forgiveness. I am reminded of Jesus on the cross saying in Aramaic, 'Father, forgive them for they know not what they do.' The act of unconditional forgiveness is love."

Jack Scalia, Actor

"Love is forgiveness and putting someone else's happiness ahead of your own."

Mike Piazza, Best-hitting catcher of all time

"As a jeweler, I see many facets of love every day as I meet with my clients. Jewels have inspired multiple metaphors of love by writers through the centuries.

The incredible gems, crystals and precious metals that are gifts from our planet are most often the result of intense temperature, pressure and time. Not the most romantic elements! I believe the most important step we must make in order to even begin to understand what love is, is to love ourselves — entirely.

Without that as our foundation, we can neither give nor receive love in all its glory and humility."

Jennifer Boin, Jeweler

⚜

"Love is a treacherous emotion — it can kill or it can cure. Though I can see where it can trap, I cannot see how it can liberate. It is, therefore, best to stay away from it.

I find it an absolute platitude, if not outright hypocrisy, for me to go around saying, 'I love' indiscriminatingly. I do not love every man. If, on the other hand, love means kindness, compassion and mercy, then I am always in love.

When opportunities arise to administer any of the above-mentioned qualities, then I give indiscriminately.

Oh, one exception: little children. I love them unconditionally."

Howard Pitterson, Artist, writer, dancer

"Love at its most basic level is the ability to be with another, physically, mentally and spiritually. And to allow their own growth process, however messy it might be, while still maintaining a connection.

It's easiest to love someone when your time spent together is more of a joyful, fun or easy connection than one of rigorous periods of personal growth.

The grace in growing your connection with another through turmoil or discomfort is the highest form of love — to see the other for the beautiful being they were created as, and to hold that belief."

Karen Gerbaz, Registered nurse

"A four-letter word. A noun. A feeling. A friendship plus passion.

A one-way street that only gives without expecting anything in return.

There's love for children, parents, friends, family, animals, religion, art, food, ice cream, chocolate, pizza, jewelry, antiques, travel, mountains, beaches, oceans, cities, romance, sensual pleasure, music and on and on.

But for me, love is that special connection with any of these that connects the object of my love and me in a deep and passionate way. I care about the person or the thing unselfishly. My satisfaction comes in spending time and energy getting to know and appreciate their qualities. And I hope to enjoy the beauty they bring into my life.

Love is unconditional acceptance of the good and not so good about your loved ones. It's more than a social relationship. More than a passing acquaintance. More than a fad or a fling. It is the 'real deal.'

It's passion and commitment. That is the story of love."

Fran Freedman Bloom, Attorney, publisher

༄

"Love is: having someone's back without them asking, having the strength to give someone what they need whether they like it or not, no matter how nasty they can get.

And always caring for them even when you don't like them at the moment."

Linne Podrat, Teacher, coach

"Love is what makes this journey worthwhile. Love is the flowing, the outpouring, the rendering from the heart and soul of emotional goodness — to myself first, and then to others. It's a feeling, a sensation, a knowingness that I get when I look in the mirror and embrace the magnificence of who I truly am.

It's the sensation I get when I am with my children and have a chance to look them in the eyes and really connect with them on a profound, deep level.

Love is an energy and an essence. A place I can always come back to when my dark side decides it wants to take over.

Love is mysterious and beautiful. It's something that can't be taken from me."

Erik Larson, CPA

"Without doubt, I'm the only woman on the planet to spend her 54th birthday enjoying the delirious consequences of weaning a teething baby while under house arrest in the jungle capitol of the military dictatorship that continues to imprison the 1991 Nobel Peace Prize Winner, Aung San Suu Kyi, for the past 18 years.

No big deal, really, since suffering is the first requirement of the job description for both my careers: mothering and humanitarian journalism.

Humanitarian is a sticky word, attracting polite grimaces and saintly visions of Mother Teresa and Warren Buffet — two names that seldom, except in some sick minds on *Jeopardy,* appear in the same sentence.

People regard 'older mothers' with the same confused reverence. They clutch their wallets and examine me with a mixture of shock and awe, wondering if my off-hours are spent on lithium or ranting on street corners. Myanmar, Dharamsala, Afghanistan, Iraq, Rwanda, pre-Madonna Malawi — most educated adults can't locate the places where I work on a marked map, which often fits the second requirement of my job description. The third requirement is that I go there so you don't have to. Then I describe the devastation and don't get paid unless it reads like a Club Med brochure.

Why do I do it? People frequently ask that question and I often ask myself the same thing, especially during 3 a.m. feedings or walking the streets of Kabul. Since any sane explanation does not apply, I choose to blame my entire, inexplicable life on Mary Martin.

I was seven years old when Peter Pan soared before my eyes. No Wendy envy and shadow-mending for me. That matinee idol set my imagination free and ruined any future I had as a seamstress.

Nothing has held me down since: not marriage, past or present; four kids; State Department warnings, nor leaking breasts. Dull does not apply. I've been dodging bullets for 10 years and giving birth for four decades.

Dying on the job doesn't seem to bother people, since fate can hit you with a garbage truck. But to some, having a baby in your 20s, 30s, 40s and 50s sounds like a bad habit, right up there with chewing cigars or scrubbing grout with your toothbrush.

Why have a baby at 53? Maybe for the same reason Flannery O'Connor offered interviewers when asked why she wrote: 'I'm good at it.' Or as the poet John Ashberry answered, 'Because I want to.' More accurately, because my husband wanted to, desperately, his whole life, and reproductive technology didn't overtake his fertility challenge until we were in our last laps around the track. If we wanted my husband's biological child, our choices were two: in-vitro (IVF in baby-making lingo) or a surrogate.

Every 10 minutes, AIDS makes an African orphan. How could we justify spending $50,000 to accomplish something that usually took 10 minutes and a couple of beers? For that price, we could buy an entire village of orphans in Guatemala. Besides, the best fertility clinics gave 'over 40' IVF pregnancies 25 percent chance of success — 15 percent after 45.

The research money and categories wisely stopped there. Why not just go to Vegas? Gambling would be a hell of a lot more fun and we might come home with a few bucks instead of burp cloths and a rectal thermometer. The odds and our sane friends were against it.

Outwardly, my husband and I were the quintessential boomer couple, the perfected illusion of acting younger and thinner than our driver's license photos. And I already had three great kids who were old enough to make me a grandparent. True, we were still sharp, attractive and enjoyed sex often and without pharmaceutical assistance — but secretly, I had begun to worry I might toss the baby in the air and forget to catch him. One does not do this with anything that cost $50,000.

Tick, tick, tick…I swear I could hear my biological clock even though the battery was dead. Weeks of vacillation turned to three

months and my husband began to squint his eyes when he looked at me, as if he suspected I wouldn't give him a kidney if needed. Transplant, I reminded him, left a much bigger scar.

By comparison and because I loved him to destruction, temporarily carrying around 25 pounds to deliver seven pounds of all he'd ever wanted seemed a small sacrifice.

Tick, tick tick...I told myself I knew what I was doing. Assured myself I wasn't crazy. Some days, I still believe it — especially when I'm nuzzling the soft folds of my tiny son's neck. His skin smells as I imagine clouds in heaven might, full of vanilla and wonder. And he smiles constantly, at everyone, reminding me of the Dalai Lama, except when he bashes his head on the coffee table. (As a footnote: the Dalai Lama vicariously introduced me to Lexie, the author/editor of this book.)

Looking back, my grown children provided me the assurance, humility and joy to know the rewards were worth the challenges and risks of parenting from the beginning, yet again.

A baby is a reminder as bold as headlines from Baghdad or Wall Street that the world is an eternity of sharp edges. To love a child or anything so much is courageous and ridiculous. Fear steals your breath away then hope swells you drunk with gratitude. Every day is a bungee jump. The intensity either kills you or saves your life on a daily basis. But on we go, having and loving and giving like there is no nuclear tomorrow.

And what choice do we have? 'What do you plan to do with your one wild and precious life?' asks the poet, Mary Oliver. How better to affirm your existence?

Be like my baby and the Dalai Lama.

Smile until your cheeks ache.

Take the chance. Take a stand.

Tell the truth.

Spread the love.

Volunteer in Darfur.

Recycle everything.

Do anything but nothing.

The world is a dangerous place to have a heart, but you can't live without one."

Karen Day, Journalist

"Love, the closest emotion and most tangible expression of God found within each human being, affects and connects us all.

Love is magical and mysterious — with a twisted sense of humor like that of a jokester.

Love is the brightest sun in the summer sky, and the biggest moon on a gorgeous evening in the fall. It's the smallest of snowflakes gently falling on a child's nose, and the very first tear of a newborn baby.

Love is the glimmer in a father's eye as he sees his son hit a home run, and the smile that just won't fade from a mother who just witnessed her daughter's first ballet recital.

Love is a gift to be treated with the utmost care like the finest stemware or best porcelain china ever made. Love is elusive and independent. It comes in and out like a wave kissing the salty shoreline and retreating — leaving traces, lingering like an original thumbprint.

Love can be painful, hurtful and a tease. It can change your life in a millisecond. And it can save your life in a blink of an eye."

Heidy Quintero, Marketing, graphic design

❧

"Love is knowing you spent your life as a good husband and good father. When all is said and done, being good at both is what life and love is all about."

John Goodman, Publicist

"A tingly feeling in your tummy. Fresh-baked chocolate cookies. Bubble baths. Mommies.

The way my dog looks at me. Children's laughter. 'Your Song' by Elton John. High school football games in the fall. The beach in the summertime. Family holidays together. New babies and old ladies.

The person you want to see after a wonderful or horrific day."

Katherine Bobo Lauber, Teacher

"Love is thinking of someone constantly.

Love is always forgiving. Love is being self-less for another, to keep them happy. Love is respect, honesty and not being able to live without someone.

Love is caring for someone, sharing, laughing, arguing, touching, hugging, crying and always being there."

Kim Passero, teacher

"Love is genuinely wishing for someone to be happy — to the point of doing everything in your power to make it that way."

Jennifer Tchinnosian, Journalist

"I wrote this to my husband on Valentine's Day in 1992:

What is love? Love isn't that bright day in June with the white tulle and champagne. But the years that follow when you've lived through it all: the fun, the joy and the pain.

Love isn't the compliments heaped on the cook when she makes that fabulous meal. But the man who eats that day-to-day fare that really has no appeal.

Love isn't the public show of hugs and kisses and affections. But the man whose touch or smile or nod goes unnoticed, without detection.

Love isn't that jeweled necklace that came as a Christmas gift. But the man who washed my hair when my arms were too tired to lift.

Love isn't the praise that is spoken so easily, and in every relation as must. But the man who holds his tongue when those words would have broken a trust.

Love is all the mundane things, big and small, that couples say and do.

And that is why I wrote this poem, to say that I love you."

Kitty Finneran, Private school administrator

"Love is the final resting place of the soul, after the noise of conflict, fear and separation has ceased to exist."

Linda Noble Topf, Writer, author, creative director

"Love is more than a sense of humor. It's more than financial generosity.

Love is respect and real intimacy, trust and honor. Love is loyalty to your family and understanding that we are only human, and not divine."

Louisa Goldsmith, Sommelier

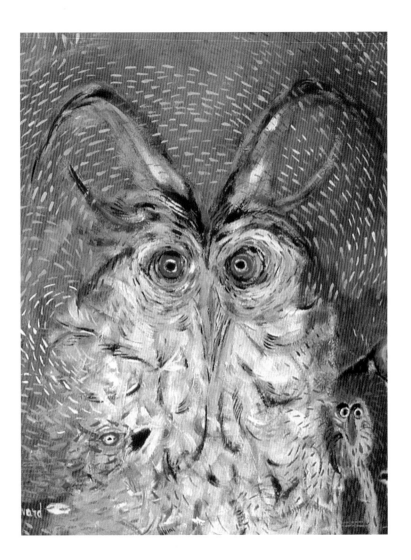

"Love never dies a natural death. It dies because we don't know how to replenish its source. It dies of blindness and errors and betrayals. It dies of illness and wounds; it dies of weariness, of witherings, of tarnishings."

Anais Nin

"The truth about love.

Love is first a feeling, then it becomes a choice. You're in Love because you chose love and choose it again.

Choose long enough and some day love just becomes who you are.

You don't have to feel love or choose love. You can just be Love."

Lynn Hoffman, Novelist

꽃

"Love inhabits every beat and breath of our existence when we are filled with grace.

Love embraces us through our gentle kindness and compassion.

It's a warm hug. It radiates our souls with an inner and outer glow. Love dances in our eyes and our passionate burning hearts. Love is living life with an open heart.

It sparkles through the joyful happiness of a child, and through the eyes of our treasured animals. It radiates from the beauty of flowers, butterflies and rainbows. Love floods our heart through the luminosity of laughter and tears.

Love is hiking through the bounteous beauty of God's artwork of nature, the voice in the wilderness, the abundant silence of a star-studded sky.

It's caring for our planet — walking hand in hand with a blossoming heart and being alive with our inner smile."

Kristina Hurrell, Life coach

"Love is a feeling that is so very sweet. When shared with another, life becomes complete.

Love is doing activities that one enjoys. For me it's playing bridge, tennis and with toys.

When I think about love, I always smile. It makes living worthwhile."

Fern Herman, School counselor

"Love is trust. Love is putting yourself in someone else's shoes. It's releasing your wildest dreams, truths and fears onto another's soul. Love is a balancing act — staying true to yourself. It's opening up.

Love is risky. Love is hiking up the highest mountains, flying into the unknown and holding hands whenever and wherever. Love is sharing a bowl of whole wheat noodles and giving your beloved the last bite. It's making room and building something together — taking turns, listening deeply and high fives for doing something without expecting anything in return.

Love is dancing with eyes closed and hands held. It's sweet, tender kisses in any season under streetlights on a city corner. It's caring for something together and watching it grow — learning from one another, and willing to teach one another.

Love is best shared."

Lesley Grill, Educator

"Love is the force that makes us take care of one another. It's the reason for getting up in the middle of the night to take care of a sick child, or driving an extra hour at the end of a long day because you know the person you're going to see needs your hug more than anything on earth.

It's the reason we cook extra-special dinners, or the little gifts we bring home 'just because.'

Love is what holds us together when everything else says, 'Run away.'

It's the reason we stay and work through the difficult nights filled with misunderstanding and pain, fear and anger. It's the glue that says, 'This is worth it' when an easier path appears next to the bumpy one we're on at the moment.

It's the reason why noticing the pretty face or attractive body of a stranger doesn't mean taking their hand or their phone number.

Love is what sometimes keeps us silent.

It's the reason we don't say that hateful word we know will wound a tender soul. The reason we remain quiet when we are tempted to ridicule dreams, tear down plans or remove hope. It's the reminder that just quietly listening is sometimes the most powerful thing we can offer someone.

Love sometimes makes us speak up. It's the reason we stand up for someone when we know they deserve it, and even more so, when we think they're wrong. It's the power behind a mom defending a child from a sharp-tongued relative; a husband defending his wife from the harsh judgment of a neighbor, or a big

sister standing up for her little sister on the playground.

Love is doing, feeling, laughing, crying, sitting, walking, trying, holding — and sometimes, letting go."

Lindsay Richardson, E-commerce program manager

"Love is the spark that ignites all life."

Hinton Harrison, Artist, author

✿

"Love is being patient with older relatives, knowing that one day that will be you.

Love is getting down on the floor and playing cars or horsey with your grandchild when arthritis makes it hard to even walk.

It's making breakfast for your son and his friends at 1 a.m. because they're hungry — but you have to get up for work at 6 a.m.

Love is letting your dog go when he's in pain — telling him how much you love him, and how you appreciate all he did for you.

It's giving your children food for their homes when it will leave you with nothing.

It isn't getting mad when something you've had forever breaks. It's just a thing, but your child is a piece of your heart.

Love is going to work when your father is dying because he believed that the students you were teaching mattered. That they had their futures ahead and you needed to help them get a high school diploma.

It's letting your child make mistakes even when it rips your heart out.

Love is sharing life with your best friend, laughing and never saying anything to the other. You just know what they're thinking."

Kristina Anne Bauer, Teacher

"Love is an everyday, conscious commitment — with yourself and others — to maintain a connection to the source of love, God Himself. It's a commitment to be patient with oneself, to volunteer your time, skills and resources to the people that surround you every day. To be the best you can and give the most of you to others. It's getting to know that the purpose and plan for your life covers more than just your life, but the people surrounding you."

Lorena Cucalon, Teacher

75

"Forgiveness is choosing to love. It is the first skill of self-giving love."

Mohandas K. Gandhi

"When we feel love and kindness toward others, it not only makes others feel loved and cared for, but it helps us also to develop inner happiness and peace."

H.H. the Dalai Lama

"The good life is inspired by love and guided by knowledge."

Bertrand Russell

"Being that love is such a subjective and cliché term, it becomes a very broad and open-to-interpretation term. I believe love is a feeling of satisfaction towards someone or something.

Focusing on love towards a person, I believe this emotion brings warmth and strength. The world may be falling on you, but because of this love everything is okay. It's the need to want to share everything (whether bad or good) with this person. It's caring about what he or she feels. It's wanting their opinion, the acceptance of the other person — with all of the virtues and defects.

Love is such a powerful feeling that it's so overwhelming. It's like a strong breeze of wind that wraps you up and makes you feel like you are floating around and you can just let go of anything and everything else."

Laura Tobon, Student

"Love isn't a simplistic thing, but to put it simply, I believe love is present when there is trust and a person is open to the connection of another spirit.

Actions can be loving when you have compassion and care for the soul of another being. I can feel complete peace and love when I'm open and connected to the light and warmth of everything in the universe.

It can feel like my soul has wings to fly — and there are no boundaries to confine me. Love is vulnerable, free, open, light and omnipresent. Love is contagious and grows when cared for.

Love is a gift to be shared."

Lee Parkhurst, Real estate broker

"Love is being there even when you do not have to be.

It's about action and about words, inclusion and remembrance. Love is the little things you do every day for someone.

Love is a balancing of life — yours and someone else's. It's like dancing, leading and following.

Love is long-term.

Love is giving of yourself in ways you never thought possible. It's saying you are sorry and meaning it.

Love is a feeling inside your heart that you can't explain because you don't know how it got there in the first place."

Linda Johnson, School administrator

"Love is the closeness felt by a loved one's touch — a spouse's hand in your hand, a dog's head in your lap and a child's quiet snuggle on the couch.

As my third grade son continues to get older, I am slow to make the transition of acceptance that hugs and kisses from his mother aren't for public viewing, particularly not in front of his classmates and friends. So, I've learned the significance of a smile, a slight wave and if we're standing near each other, a lean. As long as I don't blow kisses or try to straighten out his hair. This is where the kitchen comes into play.

Love can come through with the closeness of a simple touch, a squeeze of the hand, a hug in the kitchen, or a resting dog at your feet.

Sometimes, that simple act of love can last all day."

Kristine Lisi, Fundraiser

"Love is a feeling that I get when I give my kids a hug and I think to myself, I don't remember my life before I gave birth to you, and I can't imagine my life without you.

Love is the feeling that I get when I see my kids smile, seeing them playing together and laughing with each other.

Love is my three children, Olivia, Morgan and Connor."

Donna Wagner, Legal and personal assistant

"Love is the most mystifying, complex, powerful, extraordinary, amazing force in the universe.

Mystics have tried to capture its essence. Poets have attempted to explain it. And lovers through the ages have gotten lost in its sacred presence and its sometimes-terrifying grip.

Love is the very essence of who we are. It's where we come from, and where we return to when our time on this planet is through.

Love is what we feel when our hearts are open and our souls are free.

Love is the energy of elation and completion."

Laurie Sue Brockway, Reverend, author, editor

"As a marriage and sex therapist I spend much of my days examining this question with my patients.

First off, there are different types of love. There is familial love, that which takes place between parent and child or other family member. There is platonic love, that which takes place between friends. And there is romantic love, that which exists between two people in an intimate, sexual and unique way.

I will speak to the romantic love. Love is an extreme. It can ignite feelings of grandiosity and ecstasy when it is at its peak; when it's at its low, it can foster feelings of pain, despair and illness.

The exact same emotion can incite polar-opposite human experiences depending on how it is manifesting. After years of working with couples in crisis, I know what love is not. It is not a savior, it does not conquer all and it does not make a relationship function. Love, instead, is a catalyst for making effortful attempts to be considerate, kind and truthful.

Love is a motivator to be your best self for someone. It is a motivator to put in the work to make a relationship happen.

It is a feeling of excitement and care towards another person with whom you want to share time. Love is the experience of caring and being cared for in a singular and unique way. It is an experience that exists within oneself that makes you want to examine and explore another person to the fullest extent possible."

Lisa Abbie Paz, LMFT, PhD, Marriage and sex therapist

"Love is powerful, compassionate, ever giving, without limitations.

Love is your husband telling you that you're beautiful when you first wake in the morning and are not looking beautiful.

My children's laughter as they play with each other. Your friends reaching out and helping you when you need it but don't necessarily know you need it.

Love is when your parents reach out and give you exactly what you need when you're too guarded as an adult to ask.

It's giving back to those people and giving to others when they need it."

Lisa Kilby, Mother

"Love requires trust in the universe that we are meant to be here now, living our lives, and that all will be okay. By having this trust, we aren't afraid to give of ourselves to our families and friends.

To feel alive is to feel love. Love is the energy in our thoughts, our prayers and in our actions and reactions that makes us cherish the world, our bodies, our children and all of those close to us. Love makes the mountains majestic and the ocean mesmerizing, no matter how much time is spent near them.

Once we understand this, it's an endless and infinite gift."

Mary Bright, Mother, business owner

"Love is unconditional. For many years I have said to my children, nieces, nephews and students, 'I love you no matter what.' I have tried to live and love in such a way that they believe it. It has helped them countless times.

There are many more examples of children who have felt and known my unconditional love. One is a child who spent two years in my first grade classroom. He needed reassurance that I would continue to be his advocate. He has psychological, emotional, academic and medical issues and has depended on coming to my classroom for a hug and pep talk. People become frustrated with his quirks, but he knows I accept him as he is and he is so lovable.

My 25-year-old niece is suffering from paranoid schizophrenia and she has asked that I take a lead role in her care. She has not accepted her illness and requires lots of monitoring. In lucid moments she reminds me of my promise to 'love her no matter what.' I find comfort in knowing that she is calmed and assured by that very real sentiment.

Children benefit from knowing that our love is not payment but inherent."

Marie Milano, Teacher

❦

"Love is forgiveness."

Stephen Baldwin, Actor

"Corinthians says it all: 'Love is kind and patient, never jealous, boastful, proud, or rude. Love isn't selfish or quick tempered. It doesn't keep a record of wrongs that others do. Love rejoices in the truth, but not in evil.' "

Marcos Rodriguez, Media

"For me, love waxes and wanes in all relationships except for one: the mother-child relationship. This love began the moment I found out I was pregnant; and when I thought it could go no deeper, the love intensified the moment my children were born. And it has never waned, not once.

Sure my children can be exhausting at times, frustrating at times. Their actions can anger me at times but the love I feel for them really, truly never diminishes. It is the ultimate 'unconditional love' example. It is the most amazing, deeply felt emotional feeling I have ever experienced, and I experience it every single day.

How blessed am I?"

Lysa Reed, Mother, actress

"Love is the choice to extend oneself to another for his or her personal growth and happiness. The ability to love is a choice and it extends far beyond any sadness of misfortune that life presents to us.

The choice of love recharges and reinvigorates a person because it feeds our nature. This love can be given to a partner, a child, an elderly person, to plants and animals, and to people in general. It has the power to validate through its own nature a pure energy of goodness."

Maria E. Somarriba, Finance broker

"Love is about vital relationships. It's the engine of life. It's intimately tied to self-concept and self-awareness. It's both an emotional tie and a social tie.

I suspect most people hear the word love and think of a romantic connection because love describes an ideal way of being that we yearn for. On one hand, we hope for someone in our life who recognizes and supports who we wish to be. On the other hand, we desire someone who loves us as we are.

Love is intimately connected to its opposite — hate. Perhaps most hate is about love failed, or not achieved. Certainly both love and hate control the direction of our lives.

But love is the fundamental force. Hate is the flip side of love and cannot exist independently."

Marti Fenton Koleski, Artist

"Love is where your heart is. It comes in many sizes and shapes. It's unconditional. It's always ready to lend a helping hand and expects nothing in return. It makes life easy if it's kept simple.

Treat people in your life just as you would like to be treated.

Each person is a child of God and we need to see the face of our maker in each and every one. When given the chance, people really want love and peace in their lives.

Love needs compromise once in a while."

Mary Ann Powell, Teacher

"Where love rules, there is no will to power; and where power predominates, there love is lacking. The one is the shadow of the other."

Carl Jung

"For me, love is something for which I am immensely grateful. Love is my children. Love is my family."

Heidi Zuckerman Jacobson, Art museum director

"Love is a feeling that needs to be nurtured in order to grow. People may love someone or something as a reason to exist. It is a feeling of connection between people and other people, people and places, people and animals or in some unfortunate cases, between people and things.

People could not live without love as it gives us a reason to be alive. As people get older their definition of love changes.

For children, love is a feeling of security. For teenagers, love is a feeling of belonging. Young adults fall in love, become independent and find love in someone else.

For grandparents, love is a feeling of pride and fulfillment; their children have grown, fallen in love and through love have given life to another generation.

I feel that love is all around. Without love, things could not exist. A love for one's profession and for one another makes architects build cities, farmers plant, doctors heal, lawyers defend, teachers spread their knowledge, religions preach, mothers protect and humans live.

Bearing all this in mind, for me, love is life."

Myriam Palacios, Teacher

"Love is all there is.

Pure love radiates as compassion, free of ego. Cultivating universal love requires us to accept all that is, unconditionally and without attachment. This open love requires us to let go of all expectations from everyone in our world: our spouses, lovers, children, friends, teachers, leaders and even our guru and spiritual beliefs.

It's taking a free-fall plunge into the ocean of joy, sorrow and forgiveness. With absolute trust and self-confidence we remain open to life's gifts and lessons, all of which are found on the path of love."

Nancy Spears, Author, CEO

"Elie Wiesel says that hate is not the opposite of love. Indifference is the opposite of love.

So love is a connection between and among people, but not merely an emotion, however powerful. The first characteristic of love is that it connects us to others.

Buddhist texts tell us that love is the very fundamental wish to avoid pain and have pleasure. It begins with oneself and gradually extends to the point where we feel sentient to others the way a mother feels toward her child. So the second characteristic of love is deep empathy for others.

The philosopher Rumi beautifully writes that love is the longing for the beloved. It's not about ownership or even about union. Loving means breaking one's heart, because so long as our hearts aren't broken, we are too filled with ourselves. He calls this love an intoxication with the beloved.

The Torah teaches us to love 'with all your heart, with all your strength, with all your might.' Love is emotional. Love requires commitment, resolve and intelligence.

We need to really know what is best for the other before we presume to give to the other."

Nathan Katz, Professor of religious studies

❦

"Love is the ever-present energy that binds us all."

Kelly Smith, Founder, Center for Living Peace

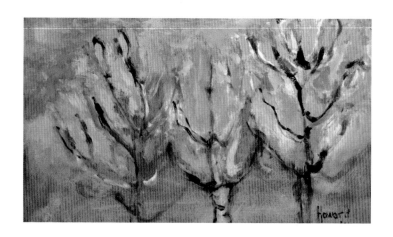

"To know love is to understand that you'll get hurt, you'll hear things you would rather not hear and you won't receive what you would wish to receive — from family, co-workers and lovers. Still, your heart is happy to be of service to them.

To love is to give, with honesty and integrity, what others need. To love is to give your best: a kind word, a smile, a helping hand. It's having a non-judgmental attitude towards others because you understand that we are all in the same boat."

Mercedes Herrera, Educator

"Love is anything or anyone that makes you feel special."

Laurie Frampton, Teacher

"Love is what happens to your heart when you feel un-sprung by the beauty, friendship or spirit of another person.

Sometimes love arrives when you least expect it. You can't believe the overwhelming sense of elation and happiness you feel."

Michele Radke, M.A., Reading specialist

❧

"Love is the true meaning of life. We wouldn't be here if not for love. When people ask, 'What's it all about?' I answer, 'Love.' Love is what life is all about."

Mary Martin, High school counselor

❧

"Love is caring about someone and caring about how they feel about me. It involves many things: the freedom to be who they are, the opportunity to grow even when it means making mistakes.

It's performing acts beneficial to them, but not smothering them; voicing concern for their choices, but not controlling them. It's making them accountable for their choices while not criticizing them. It's respecting their opinions.

Love is appreciating what they do for us, and thanking them for doing it.

It's giving when we think we have nothing left to give."

Melody Louise Posivak, Registered nurse

"Love is unconditional acceptance of the individual and non-attachment to moments shared."

Kristeen Parkhurst, Yoga therapist

"Love is the light of truth.
Stand proud brave heart.
Rejoice with love.
I am open. I am free.
Liberation pleasures the heart.
Love opens life. Our ultimate gift to share.
Love gives…ears open…minds share."

Lynnea Elkind, Poet

"Love is a stirring deep inside that allows us to feel. It allows us to feel every emotion imaginable. It justifies what we are and who we are.

Love makes a child feel secure and validated from birth to death. Love is what we search for. When we're lucky enough to find it, we nurture it and watch it grow. It brings us joy and fills the void caused by loss.

Love, a feeling worthy of sharing with the world."

Luba Kwoczak, Teacher

"A thousand half-loves must be forsaken to take one whole heart home." — *Rumi*

John Suitor, Headmaster

"Love is when you have the last child tucked into college and you feel like you are back in college, living with your boyfriend again."

Paula Prikyrl, Teacher

"Love is caring about someone without expecting anything in return."

Mary Ellen Walker, School counselor

"Love sparkles in someone's eyes. Love smiles. Love sounds like smooth and silky jazz, or maybe the snow falling after dark. It's a song.

Love is a newborn baby. Love fills the church at a wedding — and at a funeral. Love is a hug, or a handshake. Perhaps, love is a lie. Love is sweet and fresh, like strawberries picked from the vine.

It's mellow and aged, like a fine wine. Love can shine during the day or twinkle at night. Love rains down God's blessings.

Obviously, love can be foggy; but eventually the sun burns the clouds away and then we see love, like a beautiful day."

Michele Gettings, Educator

"Love is many things because there are many different kinds of love. There is love of G-d, love for parents, love for siblings, love of friends, love of a sweetheart, love of a spouse, love of children.

There is also universal love, love of mankind, love of an ideology, love of freedom. There is also love of things — cars, books, movies, TV shows, sports and music.

The truth is, love is all of these things, and all the above are like pieces in a jigsaw puzzle. So, in reality, we can't know really what love is until we reach the end of our path."

Moshe Sussman, Attorney, massage therapist

"Love is strength you obtain from loved ones and true friends. It is how you feel about yourself, others and most of all, God. It comes from within and spreads like glitter on all that you touch when it is for real."

Naeemah Overton-Houston, New teacher coach

"I polled a few of my 'helpers.' My twenty-something friend responded, 'Love is honest.' My thirty-something friend responded, 'Love is unconditional.' My nine-year-old daughter piped up with 'It is peaceful... happiness.' Her 10-year-old friend said with conviction, 'Love is life.' Her guy buddy from school thought a moment and answered, 'Isn't that when two people really like each other a lot?'

My forty-something husband answered, 'It's the feeling you get when you stare into your love's eyes... mmm...or when you watch your 16-month-old smash things and he's just loving it.'

My seventy-something mom said, 'Love is a selfless, unconditional opening of your heart — and it's usually painful.'

I guess my best definition would have to be that love is having permission from the people in your life to give and receive thoughts and experiences just like these.

Oh, if only words could do it justice."

Olivia Daane Reische, Poet

✿

"Love is something I really like.

Love is bigger than liking. Love is not something you can buy, but is something that comes out from your heart.

Love makes my heart feel big and strong."

Mia Yara, Age 7

"Love is the natural state of all things, the energy that causes everything to vibrate at its own frequency, creating integrity, authenticity, wholeness and harmony.

When there is love, the whole becomes more than the sum of the parts, and all of the parts transcend to a higher level. The energy force of love binds together all that is and all that potentially can be so that every element vibrates in synchronization with everything else.

Loving is the key that unlocks the door to our full potential and raises us to its highest possible point of being. Love can create healing, peace, beauty, truth and perfection.

At those moments our mind, body and spirit come together and open us to higher dimensions, raising us to even higher levels than we could have ever imagined."

Patricia Ann Hill, Transpersonal psychologist, TV producer

"Love is a feeling that comes from deep inside our hearts. When you realize that you can do anything for a person without necessarily having to benefit from them.

Love has several colors. But the one between a husband and wife is best when they are in love with one another.

Love is an action, and we have to work on it every day to nurture it so it grows and doesn't wither."

Robert Kalyesbula, Medical doctor

"You can give it, be in it, make it, become it, feel it and then there is the act of it. Is love an action or a description? It's both.

Life knows love though it isn't only for the living. Those who have passed on are still loved. It's their love that allows us to find peace when missing those that have passed on.

It only takes a minute to recognize once one has fallen in love. It's a deep emotion that feels good, right, wanting to go on and on, to grow between two. It causes feelings of happiness, security and lust. It's based on trust, understanding, communication and the giving of oneself selflessly.

I am loved, in love and have been loved; therefore I have lived."

Paula Mann, Special education teacher, reading specialist

"Love is a feeling that comes from profoundly appreciating another person's goodness. You can make it happen or strengthen it by focusing on the goodness in another.

If you see the divinity in another — four-legged creatures included — you'll love them passionately."

Petrina Fisher Wells, Public relations and marketing executive

"Love is Hebrews 13:3 from the Holy Bible."

Iris Marisol Green, Student

"Love at first sight is easy to understand; it's when two people have been looking at each other for a lifetime that it becomes a miracle."

Amy Bloom

"When a mother observes her child, all other sounds, movements or distractions cease to exist in her world. She is captured in the miracle.

That is love in its purest form."

Nina Saslove, Wife, mother

⚘

"Love is a feeling of not wanting to live without that other person in your life. It's always wanting to make up after a fight before you close your eyes to go to sleep.

Love is being able to forgive even when your mind tells you to run.

Love is complex, but it's what makes us whole."

Paula Brockway, Housewife

⚘

"Love is a gut feeling that you would do whatever it takes to bring happiness to someone else.

You have an understanding of what that person wants and needs, and you're willing to sacrifice a portion of your happiness to bring them joy, if needed."

Patrick Wade, Kindergarten teacher

"In the beginning, romantic love is like a white rose. It's beautiful, new, bright and exciting — without any blemishes. It isn't possible to keep the rose completely white for a lifetime. Though you try by working hard and making it a priority.

Eventually, the rose becomes dirty and it's no longer perfect. The dirtier the rose becomes, the more difficult it is to remove the dirt and make the rose white and beautiful again. You then have a choice; either discard the rose and look for a new white rose, or decide that even with imperfections, you love the rose and you will overlook them.

When you find a perfect new white rose, you might have expectations that your rose will remain white forever. You'll be disappointed and most likely in time resentful.

Love can be more fulfilling if you realize that if you find another perfect white rose, it, too, would eventually become dirty because nothing stays perfect forever."

Rebecca Mogel, Special education teacher

"Love is a universally innate and natural response among living creatures to care deeply for their offspring, and for another person or persons to whom they have a deep attraction.

It's expressed in many ways, and causes deep bonds among living organisms."

Preston D. Feden, Professor

"Love is being able to know without speaking."

Jo Ann Caplin, Professor

"Love, true love — all-encompassing, soul-rendering, ego-shattering love — is wild, violent and subversive. It undermines our sense of autonomy, separateness and alienation — the vital ingredients necessary to maintain the egocentric illusion of an isolated and independent self. It drives us mad, overwhelming body, heart and mind in an intoxicating ecstasy.

True love is a drunken insanity that makes fools of those who breathe deep its perfume.

Such love has nothing to do with Hallmark cards, dating or puppies. It isn't as easy as falling off a log, but as all-consuming as tossing one on a fire. It has nothing to do with now and forever, for time ceases in this love.

It has nothing to do with sickness and health, for death is the embrace of this love. It has nothing to do with poverty and wealth, for all owning is irrelevant in this love. This is a searing love that burns away the dross of self and selfishness.

It is a love too hot to touch, so you fling yourself wide-armed and embrace it in one explosive moment of combustion. It isn't safe. It never lasts. It leaves you scorched and scarred forever.

This is the love mystics have for God, and the love the faithful fear above all else. This is a love that kills. But it never kills the truth, only the lie and the false self that feeds off that lie.

This love is rare, not because we cannot find it, but because we almost always run away from it."

Rami Shapiro, Rabbi

"The gratification you feel from caring for another more than yourself. It is the oxygen for the brain and the blood for the heart."

Richard A. Sprague, Attorney

"Love is a verb, not a noun. It is the act of continuing to express compassion, forgiveness, caring and concern selflessly for those around us, and with no expectations."

Peter Feer, Consultant

"Love is trust. It is sharing experiences, ideas and feelings, knowing it's okay to be different. Love is more than just what you share with people. It's respect for life, yourself, others and the universe around you."

It takes time to develop. It requires acceptance, patience and compassion."

Patty Heydenberk, Development manager

"Love is the absence of all negativity."

Laura Buccellati, Handbag designer

"Love is a very deep feeling that can be applied to many people, places, things and ideas.

I don't believe there is just one definition of love. Knowing God's loves me provides me with feelings of trust, courage and comfort. The feeling I have for my husband and my children is love, and it is different for each of them. I love my parents, and that is different again. And I love my sister and brother, and the feeling is different for each of them.

This is the kind of love that grounds. It's like a foundation. It's the underpinnings for all the other feelings that come up. There can be joy, annoyance, comfort, anger, passion, frustration, worry, trust, and underneath it all is love.

Then, there is a whole different kind of love. I love the beach, I love Hawaii, I love cinnamon coffee cake, I love to ride my bike, I love to ski, I love the smell of my favorite perfume when I put my nose to my wrist, I love coming home, I love to read a book that takes me 'away.'

I love to laugh.

I guess the common theme in all these examples of love is that it is deep inside, where I imagine my soul to be, in a place that can't be touched, can't be seen, can't be heard, but is unquestionably there."

Robin Santoro, Guidance counselor

"Love is accepting and being accepted exactly as you are, and feeling how wonderful it is to share this."

Priscilla Glennon, Nurse

"Love is like a roller coaster. Ups and downs. Excitement. Anticipation. Scary, sometimes making you feel like you're going to throw up.

And at the end, getting in line to do it all over again."

Phillip Freed, Teacher

"In our journey through life we experience love at levels, ranging from the physical to the sublime. In its purest form it's untainted and inexpressible in words. But it's powerful and transformative.

Human nature propels us to love all sentient beings and recognize the divinity in all of them. This expression of selfless love is a state that transcends all boundaries in the physical, mental and spiritual planes, and it's blessed with infinite capacity.

Few are the mortals that truly achieve this exalted state, but many of us yearn to reach these heights in our journey."

Radha Krishnan, Engineering consultant

"The word 'love' is created by replacing the 'I' in live with a circle.

'I' symbolizes the life of the self.

'O' symbolizes the human spirit and the eternal, that which is without beginning or end and includes all possibilities.

Therefore, we can say love is when the life of the self is replaced by the eternal human spirit and all becomes possible."

Scott Moyer, Coach

"Love is that first feeling you have before all the bad stuff gets in the way.

Love is being happy and comfortable with someone and you can just be yourself — no makeup, no fancy clothes. You wake up next to them and think that you are the only two people in the world that matter. Your heart races when you see them after an hour or a day apart, and you get butterflies when they kiss you. At that moment you know you will be together forever.

To me it's always being there for the one you love and always being faithful to that person. Also, it means to accept someone for who they are and not what they have or what they do."

Saharou-dini Balarebe, Aluminum and glass man

"Love is a feeling, an action and a mindset. It's connection, caring, passion and overwhelming gratitude.

Love is the one underlying reality that keeps the darkness and the emptiness at bay. It's light, warmth and joy, even as it sometimes hurts.

Love is what keeps me going. Love is what you experience during the brief glimpses when the veil lifts from life. It's what everyone needs, and what we need more of.

Love might be nothing more than an evolutionary advantage to perpetuate our DNA, but I'm sure glad I have it, know it, feel it, act it, receive it and glory in it — especially when I'm with my kids.

I wish for love for every being."

Robin Lasersohn, Teacher

"An unconditional continuum of giving and caring."

Ileana Guelbenzu-Davis, Professor

❧

"Clearly, love is a universal teacher that meets all needs. When it's given or received unconditionally, it can eradicate loneliness, insecurity and even illness.

True love for humanity will never emit hurt and will only bring one happiness."

Richard Scalzo, Chela

❧

"Love is what you need to live, not just exist."

Marvin Hamlisch, Composer

"As I age, my view of love has come to change. Emotion and desire don't have nearly as much to do with love as I once thought. Love starts within and spreads from there.

You cannot love others more than you love yourself. Therefore, you can't forgive others more than you forgive yourself, or cherish others more than you cherish yourself, or be kinder to others than you are to yourself.

For me, love is not a spark or a bolt of lightning but more of a backdrop to life the way the sky is a backdrop to nature. The sky is in us and around us but seems to be a separate thing when we look up at it. Love is like that.

When you give love and live love you get love. There is always enough to go around, because love is like Willie Wonka's everlasting gobstopper — it never gets used up."

Tania Dibbs, Owner, Big Sky Studio

🌀

"Love is the presence of the Holy Spirit anchored firmly in my heart to live moment by moment in gentle harmony with peace and forgiveness, dissolving present doubts and future fears."

Toni Whaley, Film co-producer, executive director

"Love is the natural state of the universe. That means perfect equilibrium and absolute harmony. It is the free, unobstructed flow of the universal force. As humans, we are more or less able to allow this free flow to 'run' through us in direct proportion to our spiritual development.

The more spiritually developed we are, the more in tune with love we are, and the more we can reflect its aspects of compassion, solidarity and charity."

Wallice Jusino de la Vega, Publishing consultant

"Love is the driving force of life. Everything we do is for love of some kind.

Love of our children, love of our spouse, love of life, passions and beliefs.

Over my life I have taken true love for granted, but have come to realize how precious true love is, whether giving or receiving. I truly cherish the loves I have in my life today and I make sure the people I love are keenly aware of how I feel.

Things change fast.

Children grow and unexpected things happen. Only when we experience love to the fullest and without hesitation are we really living our life."

Trisch Hirsch, Real estate

"Love is resolving conflict and differences in a healthy, respectful way. Love is being open to your partner's point of view."

Mary Lou Castellanos, Realtor

"Love is nurturing the goodness in all sentient beings."

Molly Brooks, Wife, mother

"Love is God."

Linda Weiser, Life coach

🐇

"Love is like air or water. It looks for the invitation of space so it can fill it up. Love is the rose in my garden that bloomed this year, even though I neglected to water it. It's the traffic jam that caused me to see a little boy playing with a lizard on the side of the road. Love is the stranger who likes my laugh, even though I think it's too loud.

Love is my husband, who always sees me first when he walks into a room. It's the embrace of my friend Anna, the way Susan arranges flowers or food.

Love is my mother, who asks me to forgive her, but who forgives me without me ever having to ask. It's my sisters, who are so very different, but who spend an entire hour trying to decide what DVD to watch, not wanting anyone to be unhappy. Love is my cat, who carries a Christmas stocking up a flight of stairs because I am crying and he wants to give me something. Love was my blind friend Stanley, who taught me to fox-trot, and Annabel, who corresponded with me for years and years, agreeing never to meet because to each other we were perfect.

Love is Father Virgil, who transcended his religion to love God with me. Love was my first breath and love and will be my last."

Saral Burdette, Interfaith celebrant minister

"Love is staying strong and never giving up when your child is diagnosed with a life-threatening illness.

Love is putting your own life on hold so that your child never feels alone as they endure eight hours of daily chemotherapy for a year, followed by six weeks of radiation and arduous surgery to preserve a limb.

When the disease recurs a second and then a third time, and the treatments resume, love means making it possible for friends to visit from great distances and remaining positive in the face of continued adversity. And then, love is celebrating all of the good days, each and every one, and never taking them for granted.

Love is hugging and holding your child and being so grateful that he can hug back."

Susan Zedlacher, Teacher

"Never hearing the words 'I love you' growing up set me on a path of searching for it — in the women I befriended and in all the men I met.

Surviving drug addiction, friendship betrayals and three failed marriages, I came to know what love was not.

Gratefully, the silver lining from that phase of my life journey is my precious daughter, a darling fourth husband and a cast of soul-sister girlfriends. It is through them and my many animals that I have come to know unconditional love.

As a little girl, I remember doing a lot of daydreaming, spending hours lying on the grass and in the snow gazing up at the sky. I had the sense then that one day something big, something great, would happen to me. I've lived my life being drawn towards that 'something.'

As I approached my 55th birthday I felt like I was falling into an abyss. My hormones were flatlining, my energy level was waning and I wasn't sleeping well. Having always been somewhat vain about my appearance I became desperate to fix myself.

Little did I know that intuitively choosing the holistic path to wellness would lead me to know absolute love. On one fateful health retreat, I experienced what I have come to call my own Big Bang. In writing this I'm lost for words to truly convey the intimacy shared in that moment of Divine ecstasy. In a euphoric state of oneness every cell in my body was ignited in the recognition of my one true love...my beloved God! Fully conscious I experienced heaven on earth, my death and rebirth, now and forever more.

Having never been religious I'm still in awe that this happened to me.

I now know that 'something' I've been drawn towards all my life was my spiritual awakening, and the absolute realization that there is no separation with all that is. I am one with me, with you, with nature, with mankind, with God — it's all the same thing.

In my lifelong search for love I have come to know one thing for sure: love is a homecoming, and a return to oneself."

Ruth Schlossberg, Interior designer, writer

"When the power of love overcomes the love of power the world will know peace."

Jimi Hendrix

"Love is a promise, love is a souvenir, once given never forgotten, never let it disappear."

John Lennon

"What the world really needs is more love and less paperwork."

Pearl Bailey

"Love may have as many meanings as there are people on the earth. Buddha said, 'All of life is suffering,' and that the only way to end this suffering is to learn to see the truth.

Through meditation we pierce through the more gross or physical aspects of ourselves and go deep within us to find our 'Bliss Sheath.'

In being in touch with our inner-most selves we connect with cosmic consciousness, the 'Oneness of All Things,' 'The Tao.' From this viewpoint of awareness, uncluttered by prejudice and pre-conceived concepts, we view the world and all things in the world with open hearts and minds.

Everything is seen as 'The One.' One mind. One heart. One love."

Sally Selligman, Classical hatha yoga instructor

"Love is respected space. It doesn't possess, it doesn't attach and it doesn't hurt.

It trusts unceasingly.

Love is self-awareness, and from that place your love is shared, rather then given with expectation.

Love is who we all are.

A saying I live by: 'Love has no color, gender, religion, language or nationality.' "

Sister Jenna, Curator, meditation museum

"Where there is great love, there are always miracles."

Willa Cather

"After all these years, I see that I was mistaken about Eve in the beginning; it is better to live outside the Garden with her than inside it without her."

Mark Twain

"We have just enough religion to make us hate, but not enough to make us love one another."

Jonathan Swift

"Love is grace, forgiveness, acceptance and warrior loyalty."

Sonya Rodriguez, Wife, mother

"What is love and why does the world need so much of it now?

Love is innocence, courage, authenticity, fearlessness, feeling, compassion, mercy, honesty and accepting consequences of behavior. Love is about assuming responsibility.

It's also about vitality, forgiveness, being human, being able to feel suffering. Love is living in grace, awareness, feeling full, having no needs.

Love is inspiration.

Love is a very active state. It takes tremendous discipline to move through a day's activities just staying in the heart.

Love is, to quote Jesus, 'Being in the world, but not of the world.' Love is God. God is Love."

Sorah Dubitsky, Professor, author

"Love needs to be flexible. We have loving relationships that need flexibility. Sometimes with one person we express love by being empathic and compassionate. With others, we express love by teaching, setting boundaries and having expectations.

Some days, one person may need your love more than another.

Individuals who give love steadily often gain more than those who limit themselves. There are more opportunities to love than not to love."

Valerie Pearce, Wife, mother

"Dear God, how do I describe love in a form that best serves you? Is it possible? Help me bridge the gap between your love lens and mine.

'My dear child, love is in the eye of the beholder. Just as I see love one way — from my lens, as you say — you see it through yours. All is love — I do not discriminate as you might because my view of love does not pass through an intellect filter. It is my essence, as it is yours. Quiet your mind. Listen and feel from within. This inner space, which lies beneath the layers of the intellect, is the keeper of your essence. Acknowledge my essence merged with yours, absent the intellect filter. Be still in this place, attached to nothing and open to everything. Here, you will find love; here you will find Me.'"

Valerie Bartol, Therapist, integrative life coach

"Love is 1 Corinthians 13:4-8, New International Version.
'Love is patient, love is kind.
It does not envy, it does not boast, it is not proud.
It is not rude, it is not self-seeking.
It is not easily angered, it keeps no record of wrongs.
Love does not delight in evil, but rejoices with the truth.
It always protects, always trusts, always hopes, always perseveres.
Love never fails.'"

Vicki Smith, Special education teacher.

"Love is the willingness to persist in all affairs with others and to bring oneself to relationships.

Love is neutral when faced with unacceptable behavior in another.

Love is knowing that God is here for me no matter what.

Love is absolute faith that there is a solution, a healing to all problems.

Love is self-acceptance and thereby acceptance of others and their difficulties. Love is my willingness to have faith and be strong, even if it isn't yet.

Love for myself and others grows more as I age because my faith grows stronger. Love is my Bible.

Love is getting up off your knees, accepting and moving forward."

Starr Porter, Meditation teacher

"Love is a natural internal feeling towards oneself and others. From the perspective of Jainism, it means the universal feeling of compassion and amity towards all forms of life.

Love isn't taken as physical attraction, material happiness and something that connects to the material world with its outcome of suffering, pain and sadness.

In fact, love is a natural phenomena and the true nature of self that connects with every individual. By giving respect, honor and dignity, the flow of love will strengthen our inner mind and unite us to live happily and peacefully.

Saying 'I love you' doesn't mean 'I like you.' If there is a feeling of likeness, that means there is a feeling of unlikeness, too. Love is beyond the feelings of like and dislike because they fill our mind with negativity."

Samani Charita Prajna, Jain nun

"Love is undivided devotion, like when you leave your dog confined to the house and yard all day while you ski, and he wants to give you endless licks and kisses when you get home.

Or when you yell at your kids for tracking mud through the house and they still want to sit on your lap after dinner and cuddle with you in bed."

Stan Cheo, Physical therapist

"Love is when you put the needs of those you love ahead of your own needs and wants."

Sue O'Bryan, Attorney

"Love is understood and most sought after.
Being able to love one's self and others is influenced by how we have experienced love from our family and those close to us."

Susan Loretta, Administrator

"Love is a pure and raw element, affection and happiness rolled into a great ball of joy. It feels and looks like the warmth of the sun on a summer afternoon. Love resides in the heart but leaves frequently for great adventures and unexpected events.

Love has a sense of humor.

Love can cross space and time in the blink of an eye and can make a heart skip a beat for something ancient and long forgotten. Love binds us with family and friends beyond mortal time.

It inspires and helps build brighter futures in a better world. Love heals old wounds and is a bridge between compassion and understanding.

Love is an essential part of happiness.

As a photographer, sometimes I see love from a mile away as an energy that pulls me towards it. Other times it can be subtle and can only be distinguished by a tiny highlight in the smallest corner of an eye. It's magic to watch and I never get tired of witnessing it because love never grows old."

Thomas Bollinger, Photographer, adventurer

"Love is the way we interact with one another. A manner. A way of being. To love someone is to actively feel something and react to someone."

Wendy Lucas, Real estate broker

LEXIE BROCKWAY POTAMKIN

Lexie Brockway Potamkin brings a diverse career and extensive world travel to her work as author of *What is Love?* A human rights activist, counselor and minister, she spent many years working in the worlds of business, entertainment and media.

A former Miss World USA, she hosted her own talk show and eventually became a public relations professional working for Golin Harris Public Relations, Gold Mills Inc., and Rogers and Cowan Public Relations. At the height of her business success, having founded and sold her own PR firm, she returned to school for her Master's Degree in Applied Psychology from the University of Santa Monica. Her ensuing counseling work inspired her to the next spiritual step, becoming an ordained minister.

She has traveled the world and over the past decade has been a guiding force and inspiration for many charitable organizations. In Philadelphia, she was President of Resources for Children's Health and a trustee for the International House. Her passion for human rights has led her to speak before the United Nations as Vice President of the International League for Human Rights, and work with the Dalai Lama and Tibetan Buddhist monks.

Lexie and her husband have also founded an elementary school in Florida.

Lexie is currently working with respected teachers at The Spiritual Paths Institute. She is studying contemplative wisdom and applied spirituality, combining intellect, heart and spiritual practice. She lives in Colorado with her family, three dogs, two cats, a parrot and a few hamsters. This is Lexie's third book. She has also written *What is Spirit?* and *What is Peace?*

Susan B. Howard

Susan B. Howard combines a love of nature, color and humor to bring her unique imaginary worlds to life in oil paintings.

She left a world of crime, corruption, ugly and vile human behavior — as a successful television news producer for 10 years — to pursue her true passion, painting. In 1997, she received a Master of Fine Arts from the Pennsylvania Academy of the Fine Arts and was awarded its Fellowship Purchase Prize.

Susan's whimsical menageries have been exhibited in numerous museums and galleries, including the Susquehanna Art Museum, the Delaware Art Museum, the Berman Museum of Art and the United States embassy in Skopje, Macedonia. Her work is in scores of private collections as well as the permanent collection of the State Museum of Pennsylvania and WHYY-TV.

Susan's paintings have been praised by art critics and laymen alike. Edward J. Sozanski, art critic for the *Philadelphia Inquirer,* wrote, "Susan B. Howard is an artist blessed with an unusual gift for compelling and plausible fantasy.... Her paintings are childlike only in their range of imagination; otherwise, they're clearly the work of a trained intelligence."

Burton Wasserman, reviewing several of her solo and group exhibitions for *Art Matters* and *Prime Time Monthly,* wrote, "While

Howard deals with events and sensations that have their origins in the world of everyday experience, she intensifies their reality by employing a graphic language rich with dimensions of unanticipated invention.... In addition, and this is important, they have been superbly executed, in an unbelabored, painterly manner, with a very well-informed hand, completely in control of every brush stroke."

Anne R. Fabbri wrote in the *Philadelphia Daily News:* "Howard's paintings can be explained on many different levels. For children, they're a visual delight full of unexpected surprises, such as the perky little bird hopping a ride on a huge animal's back. Adults also enjoy the fantasy world but sense the darker side, recognizing the observer who seems to know too much about them. This is Howard the artist, a person who knows a lot about the human equation but is too tactful to reveal it all up front."

Susan lives in Villanova, Pennsylvania, with her husband and pet parrot.

Index

146